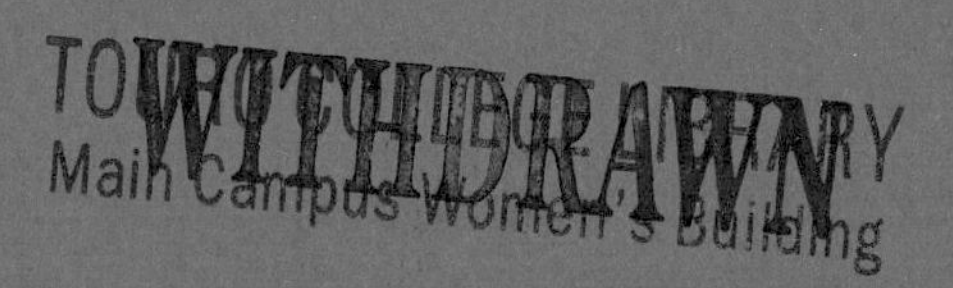
WITHDRAWN
TOURO COLLEGE LIBRARY
Main Campus Women's Building

☆

JOHN DEWEY

☆

The GREAT AMERICAN THINKERS *Series*

JONATHAN EDWARDS • *Alfred Owen Aldridge*
BENJAMIN FRANKLIN • *Ralph L. Ketcham*
JOHN WOOLMAN • *Edwin H. Cady*
THOMAS JEFFERSON • *Stuart Gerry Brown*
JOHN C. CALHOUN • *Richard N. Current*
GEORGE BANCROFT • *Russel B. Nye*
CHAUNCEY WRIGHT • *Edward H. Madden*
CHARLES PEIRCE • *Thomas S. Knight*
WILLIAM JAMES • *Edward C. Moore*
THORSTEIN VEBLEN • *Douglas F. Dowd*
JOHN DEWEY • *Richard J. Bernstein*

IN PREPARATION

ALEXANDER HAMILTON • *Stuart Gerry Brown*
RALPH WALDO EMERSON • *Warren Staebler*
THEODORE PARKER • *Arthur W. Brown*
JOSIAH ROYCE • *Thomas F. Powell*
THEODORE ROOSEVELT • *William Harbaugh*
ALFRED NORTH WHITEHEAD • *Nathaniel Lawrence*
GEORGE SANTAYANA • *Willard E. Arnett*
DR. W.E.B. DU BOIS • *Henry Lee Moon*
NORMAN THOMAS • *Robert J. Alexander*

☆

JOHN DEWEY

Richard J. Bernstein, Ph.D.
Chairman of the Department of Philosophy,
Haverford College

☆

SERIES EDITORS

Arthur W. Brown, Ph.D.
President, Adelphi University; and

Thomas S. Knight, Ph.D.
Professor and Chairman of the
Department of Philosophy, Adelphi University

WASHINGTON SQUARE PRESS, INC. • NEW YORK • 1966

Library of Congress Catalog Number: 66-16176

Published simultaneously in the United States and Canada by Washington Square Press, Inc.

Printed in the United States of America

☆

CONTENTS

PREFACE

No American philosopher has been more widely discussed and criticized than John Dewey. Yet despite this—or perhaps because of this—there is a great deal of confusion and misunderstanding about what he really believed and what is the heart of his philosophic outlook. I have tried to present a sympathetic, comprehensive statement of Dewey's intellectual vision. I believe that this is the most effective way to discover what Dewey "stood for" and, thereby, enable us to evaluate his contribution to philosophic inquiry and American thought.

Dewey frequently emphasized a genetic approach to problems. He would attempt to get back to the immediate context from which problems and ideas emerged in order to understand and evaluate them in proper perspective. Dewey did not begin with his "mature" position but gradually evolved it, over a long period, in response to new ideas and influences. Consequently, I have introduced the reader to Dewey's leading ideas by sketching Dewey's own intellectual development. This provides the context for stating what I take to be the heart of Dewey's philosophic vision—his theory of experience and the ways in which experience is related to nature. This in turn enables us to appreciate Dewey's contribution to the understanding of logic, ethics, art, education, and democracy. After completing the outline of Dewey's philosophy, I take seriously his own concept of philosophy's being the criticism of criticisms by scrutinizing his views.

I have tried to avoid a "label" approach to philosophy. The terms "pragmatism," "instrumentalism," "progressive education" appear infrequently in this book, as they do in Dewey's own writings. Dewey himself was never happy with labels and slogans. While they can sometimes be helpful in providing an orientation, they can be harmful and misleading when they prevent us from seeing what a man actually believes.

The treatment of Dewey here is both sympathetic and critical, but I do not think that these attitudes are incompatible. It is just what Dewey called for in the discussion of philosophic issues. Too much of the criticism of Dewey has been wide of the mark, and defenders of Dewey have frequently done him an injustice by adopting a patronizing attitude toward him. We do him the most justice by taking his ideas with the full seriousness that they deserve and subjecting them to critical evaluation.

I have been concerned with Dewey's thought during the past ten years. It was Charles W. Hendel and John E. Smith who originally aroused my interest in Dewey. During this time I have also received the encouragement of John Herman Randall, Justus Buchler, and George Geiger, whose work has helped us to understand the import of Dewey's thought. My wife Carol and Mr. Walter Emge have read the entire manuscript and have helped in more ways than they realize.

I have enjoyed writing this book; my hope is that it may help others to become acquainted with the breadth and seriousness of this humane thinker. A good deal of my enjoyment stems from the encouragement and prodding of my daughters, Robin and Andrea, who wanted "their" book on John Dewey completed. It is dedicated to them, for in writing it I have come to realize how much Dewey's ideas have molded their characters.

Chapter 1

PHILOSOPHY AS CRITICISM

John Dewey is known as America's most influential philosopher and educator. His name has been associated with the philosophic movement called "pragmatism" and the educational movement sometimes labeled "progressive education"—both of these movements have been more frequently abused than understood. It is acknowledged, however, both by Dewey's champions and his critics that his philosophic outlook represents a distinctive intellectual expression of American culture. But if we seriously reflect on the significance of this claim, then we must first confront some knotty problems. What do we mean by claiming that Dewey, or any other philosopher, is an "American" philosopher? Surely more is intended than to call attention to the facts that he was born in Burlington, Vermont, on October 20, 1859, grew up in New England, attended the University of Vermont and later Johns Hopkins University, spent most of his life teaching at various American universities including the Universities of Michigan, Minnesota, and Chicago, and, from 1904 until his retirement in 1930, Columbia University. As soon as we ask what is the "more" that is intended, we must ask what is the relation of philosophy to the cultural environment from which it emerges? When we speak of Greek, German, British, or French philosophy, we do think that the specific emphases, problems, methods and aims reflect what is distinctive about these various cultures. Yet, at the same time, most philosophers in the Western tradition have conceived of philosophy as primarily concerned with objective truth, as an inquiry that makes and seeks to justify basic claims about the nature of reality, thought, and action that transcend the local restrictions of time and place.

One of the most provocative features of Dewey's thought is his criticism of the concept of philosophy as a discipline primarily concerned with discovering and justifying "truths." "In philosophy we are dealing with something comparable to the meaning of Athenian civilization or of a drama or a lyric."[1] Where truth is at stake, it is all important. But philosophy is not primarily concerned with discovering and verifying truths. Given certain truths, the philosopher wants to understand their general significance, their coherence, the ways in which they alter the intellectual landscape, the ways in which they can lead us to envision new possibilities for human life. Dewey's entire philosophy may be approached as an attempt to elaborate and defend a "new" concept of philosophy. If we want to grasp the distinctive flavor of his thought, then we must become clearer about his views on the nature of philosophic inquiry.

Every philosopher who comes to grips with what he is doing must ask: Why does there seem to be so much disagreement among philosophers? What is the significance of this disagreement? Is it an indication of the futility of philosophy, or is it perhaps a sign of the soundness of philosophy? Philosophers throughout the ages have claimed that their systems and methods, once and for all, show us what we can *really* know about the nature of reality, thought and action. And they are superseded by new attempts to wipe the slate clean and start afresh. One of the few safe generalizations about the course of philosophic development is that every age will have its philosophic prophet who will proclaim that he has discovered the right way of doing philosophy—a way that will "finally" lead us from confusion and darkness to a promised land of clarity and truth. In our own time, there has been a widespread skepticism about the entire philosophic tradition—a skepticism which has occasionally hardened into a dogma. Faced with the conflicting variety of philosophic positions, some contemporary philosophers have argued that the reason for this bewildering variety stems from the failure to employ objective criteria of meaning and truth for evaluating philosophic claims. Confronted with the challenge of rapid and successful development of the sciences, philosophers have desperately attempted to delineate the true province of philosophy. We have been told that the task of philosophy is to clear up confusions that are generated from the misuse of language, or that philosophy can only describe and never explain, or that the task of philosophy is to achieve conceptual clarity. When we turn to the vital issues of politics and morality, there has been, especially in England and America, a prevailing sentiment that the philosopher's job is to describe and clarify the ways in which we actually discuss, argue, and reason about these issues. It is not the philosopher's task to tell us what we ought to do and how we ought to act.

Dewey would not have accepted any of the above as an adequate characterization of philosophy. He was at once skeptical about and respectful of the philosophic tradition. He did not believe that the purpose of philosophy is to reveal the basic structure of an eternal reality. He did not believe that philosophers have special access to a realm beyond the world in which we think and act. He was critical of the quest for certainty that had been characteristic of so much of Western philosophy. But, he did *not* believe that 2,500 years of philosophizing was based on a mistake. Every great philosophy is intimately related to the cultural environment from which it arises. It reflects the basic aspirations, perplexities, conflicts of the culture, and it seeks to give new order, coherence, and direction to what is funded in cultural experience. "The life of all thought is to effect a junction at some point of the new and the old, of deep-sunk customs and unconscious dispositions, that are brought to the light of attention by some conflict with newly emerging directions of activity. Philosophies which emerge at distinctive periods define larger patterns of continuity which are woven in effecting the enduring junctions of a stubborn past and an insistent future."[2] This concept of philosophy owes a good deal to Hegel, who exercised an enormous influence on the shaping of Dewey's outlook. But already Dewey departs from Hegel. Philosophy is not solely the intellectual expression of what is implicit in the total complex of a stage of civilization, but plays an active role in shaping the direction of civilization. The philosopher does not simply reflect the cultural tradition which he inherits: he can achieve distance and freedom from what has been and what is, and he can imaginatively envision what can be and what ought to be. The philosopher is like the artist, whose task—which is never completed —is to reconstruct the material that is taken into something that has greater form and order, something that is funded with esthetic significance. This artistic and esthetic dimension, which pervades all of Dewey's thought, has often been neglected in appraising his philosophy.

There is also a scientific aspect of philosophy. The philosophic imagination "acknowledges its responsibility to meet the logical demands of ascertained facts."[3] The philosopher has the responsibility to be constantly alert to the discovery of new scientific truths and to the development of scientific procedures. Philosophy is not a special science along with the other sciences, nor is it in competition with the sciences. The philosopher must try to understand how new developments in science alter our total intellectual landscape.

From this perspective, the diversity of philosophic positions is no cause for despair or disillusionment. If philosophy were a discipline that was primarily concerned with the discovery and verification of new truths, then the lack of agreement among philosophers on basic issues would support indictment of it. But if we think of the philosopher as a man who is struggling with the most fundamental conflicts and problems of his time in order to understand their significance and to present us with an imaginative reconstruction, then it is natural to expect diversity. This variety can be a sign of the vitality of philosophic inquiry. Not only do the specific problems and conflicts of different ages change, but there are "diverse currents and inspirations in almost every historic epoch."[4] Only when a philosopher attempts to cut himself off from the "problems of men" and conceives of philosophy as a discipline with its own unique methods and subject matter is there a danger of philosophy becoming futile and sterile.

Philosophy can be described as a form of criticism;

it is a criticism of criticisms. Criticism is not a matter of formal treatises or of making negative judgments. It is a way of understanding, evaluating, and dealing with specific conflicts. Man is a creature, who, for better or worse, finds himself in a world in which there are immediate accepted values. He is a creature whose very existence demands making choices and decisions. He can live his life uncritically accepting the values and methods which he has inherited. When faced with new problems, men can, and most men do, attempt to use old formulas and standards. Indeed, one of the thoughts that is always in the foreground for Dewey is that the natural tendency of modern technological society is to encourage passivity and docility among men. Although our powers are limited, we can become critical—our intelligence can be nurtured and sharpened so that we do exercise some control over our fate. "In knowledge, for example, there are beliefs *de facto* and beliefs *de jure*. In morals, there are immediate goods, the desired, and reasonable goods, the desirable. In esthetics, there are goods of an undeveloped or perverted taste and there are the goods of cultivated taste."[5] In each case, the difference between the immediate and the mediate is precisely the extent to which the latter is funded with intelligence and based on reasonable choice. Intelligence is not a matter of the exercise of reason by an internal act of will. Intelligence involves a complex set of habits and dispositions which can be developed and nurtured through education. As we shall see, Dewey's concept of the nature and function of education is intimately related to every aspect of his philosophy. The philosopher, then, as the general critic, is the man who engages in criticism as a way of life for the sake of instituting and securing more enduring and extensive reasonable values.

Dewey's view of philosophy can be easily parodied by saying that he thought that the function of philosophy is social reform. But Dewey's reply is that " 'social reform' is conceived in a Philistine spirit, if it is taken to mean anything less than precisely the liberation and expansion of the meanings of which experience is capable."[6] Consequently, this "new" concept of philosophy is a return to an older concept of philosophy as the love of wisdom—wisdom that is not identified with the accumulation of knowledge but cannot exist without knowledge. More specifically, Dewey's view of philosophy resembles Aristotle's concept of practical wisdom—"a reasoned and true state of capacity to act with regard to human goods."[7]

Dewey's concept of philosophy provides us with the clue for understanding (in a preliminary way) the distinctive sense in which he is an American philosopher. He was primarily concerned with what he took to be the basic conflicts in American democratic society. To understand this society, it is essential to understand how it has been influenced and shaped by older institutions and ideas. As he tells us in his *Democracy and Education,* "The philosophy stated in this book connects the growth of democracy with the development of experimental method in the sciences, evolutionary ideas in the biological sciences, and the industrial reorganization, and is concerned to point out the changes in subject matter and method of education indicated by these developments."[8] Here we have announced the major interrelated themes that set the cultural matrix for his philosophic inquiry. But philosophy in general and American philosophy in particular involves criticism and reconstruction. It does not seek to glorify or rationalize the *status quo*. In speaking of American philosophies and his own instrumentalism, Dewey says:

> They are not limited to reproducing what is worn and imperfect in this environment. They do not aim to glorify the energy and the love of action which the new conditions of American life exaggerated. They do not reflect the excessive mercantilism of American life. . . . Instrumentalism maintains, in opposition to many contrary tendencies in the American environment, that action should be intelligent and reflective, and that thought should occupy a central position in life. . . . What we insist upon above all else is that intelligence be regarded as the only source and sole guarantee of a desirable and happy future.[9]

Implicit in this concept of philosophy and the role of American philosophy are a number of key concepts and themes that demand exploration. What precisely does Dewey mean by "experience," "intelligence," and "reconstruction"? How are these concepts related to the development of democracy, experimental science, biological evolution, modern industrial society, and education? These questions and others that they suggest can best be answered by seeing how Dewey attempted to weave these various concepts and influences into an imaginative vision of what human society could become.

Chapter 2

FROM HEGEL TO DARWIN

Philosophic inquiry, freed from the fetters of theological and religious apologetics, has a short history in America. In 1835 De Tocqueville reported that in no part of the civilized world was less attention paid to philosophy than in the United States. Morris Cohen, one of the first historians of American philosophy, frankly tells us that "American philosophy before the Civil War produced not a single original philosophic work of commanding importance. To the modern reader it is all an arid desert of commonplace opinion covered with the dust of pedantic language."[1]

The intellectual event that most dramatically awoke America from its dogmatic slumber was the publication of Darwin's *On the Origin of Species by Means of Natural Selection* in 1859, the year in which Dewey was born. In its immediate impact, the theory of evolution, or rather the various popularizations and distortions of it, posed a threat to the dogmas and beliefs that prevailed among the conservative clergy. Popular books and periodicals were filled with the "conflict" between religion and science. Underlying the immediate disputes, there were more profound influences at work. The discoveries of the new biology gave an impetus to the development of the full range of social and human sciences. To many thinkers, it seemed that the experimental procedures that had proven so successful in the physical sciences would finally show the way to an intellectual understanding and control of human phenomena. Furthermore, the impressive advances in the sciences posed new problems for understanding the distinctive nature of scientific method and its significance for human knowledge. A new, tough-minded intellectual temper was emerging on the American scene. Serious scientific research mushroomed, and superseded the amateurism of the previous generation.

The founding of Johns Hopkins University (where Dewey did graduate work in philosophy) was both a cause and an effect of this new intellectual climate. The spirit of Johns Hopkins was eloquently expressed by Charles Sanders Peirce, who was teaching at Johns Hopkins when Dewey came as a student. In an address delivered in Paris on July 4, 1880, he declared:

> One university in our country, the Johns Hopkins University at Baltimore, has been carried on upon principles directly contrary to those which have governed the other colleges. That is to say, it has here alone been recognized that the function of a university is the production of knowledge, and that teaching is only a necessary means to the end. In short, instructors and pupils here compose a company who are all occupied in studying together, some under leading strings and some not.[2]

John Dewey was not only born into this environment of intellectual ferment, but by the end of the nineteenth century he became one of the leading proponents and interpreters of the new scientific environment.

In a very revealing passage from his autobiographical sketch, Dewey dates his first interest in philosophy from a course in physiology that he took during his junior year at the University of Vermont in which Thomas Huxley's *Lessons in Elementary Physiology* was the text.

> It is difficult to speak with exactitude about what happened to me intellectually so many years ago, but I have an impression that there was derived from the study a sense of the interdependence and interrelated unity that gave form to intellectual stirrings that had been previously inchoate, and created a kind of type or model of a view of things to which material in any field ought to conform. Subconsciously, at least, I was led to desire a world and a life that would have the same properties as had the human organism in the picture derived from the study of Huxley's treatment.[3]

The concept of the interacting organism that was the source of Dewey's initial interest in philosophy became the leading concept of his philosophy. Dewey's concern with the model of an interacting organism is the key for understanding his early passionate interest in Hegel and the neo-Hegelian idealists, as well as his eventual rejection of Hegel. Throughout his philosophic career Dewey returned again and again to the explication and the application of the concept of the interacting organism in order to understand man's situation in the world. Dewey had a deep intellectual and emotional aversion to what he took to be static, formal, and dualistic. He saw life in all its forms as a dynamic interplay of interrelated and interdependent elements where distinctions are functional and changing rather than fixed and static. For Dewey, it was Hegel who had given the most penetrating intellectual expression to this insight. "Hegel's synthesis of subject and object, matter and spirit, the divine and the human, was, however, no mere intellectual formula: it operated as an immense release, a liberation. Hegel's treatment of human culture, of institutions and arts, involved the same dissolution of hard-and-fast dividing walls, and had a special attraction for me."[4] We catch the flavor and spirit of the young Dewey in the following passage from one of his articles, "The New Psychology," written when he was under the spell of Hegel.

> Experience is realistic, not abstract. Psychical life is the fullest, deepest, and richest manifestation of this experience. The New Psychology is content to get its logic from this experience, and not do violence to the sanctity and integrity of the latter by forcing it to conform to certain preconceived abstract ideas. It wants the logic of fact, of process, of life. It has within its departments of knowledge no psycho-statics, for it can nowhere find spiritual life at rest. For this reason, it abandons all legal fiction of logical and mathematical analogies and rules; and is willing to throw itself upon experience, believing that the mother which has borne it will not betray it. But it makes no attempts to dictate to this experience, and to tell it what it *must* be in order to square with a scholastic logic. Thus the New Psychology bears the realistic stamp of the contact with life.[5]

This passage is typical of much of Dewey's early writing. There is a thinly disguised attack on a priori "static" categories. The cry now is, Back to experience!

but there is an implicit criticism of traditional empiricist concepts of experience. Experience is not an aggregate or blending of discrete atomic perceptions. Experience is dynamic; it is an active process. As with so much of Dewey's early writing, there is more enthusiasm in this passage than philosophic illumination. It is programmatic and suggestive rather than specific and concrete. We get a feel for what he is "against," but it is more difficult to understand clearly what he is "for." How are we to understand what he means by "experience"? What is the new "logic of fact, of process, of life"? Despite Dewey's own protest against abstract and static categories, and his insistence on the changing and the concrete, we are given very little guidance about what the latter involves.

Dewey had learned his Hegel under the guidance of G. S. Morris, his teacher at Johns Hopkins and later his colleague at the University of Michigan. Perhaps the epitome of the permanent Hegelian influence on Dewey is expressed in what Dewey said about his own teacher. Dewey seems to be passing judgment on himself when he writes:

> I should say that he was at once strangely indifferent to and strangely preoccupied with the dialectic of Hegel. Its purely technical aspects did not interest him. But he derived from it an abiding sense of what he was wont to term the organic relationship of subject and object, intelligence and the world. . . . When he talked as he was wont to do, of the mechanical and the organic, it was this contrast which stood forth. It was a contrast between the dead and the living, and the contrast was more moral and spiritual than physiological, though biology might afford adumbrative illus-

> trations. His adherence to Hegel (I feel quite sure) was because Hegel had demonstrated to him, in a great variety of fields of experience, the supreme reality of this principle of living unity maintaining itself through the medium of differences and distinctions.[6]

Dewey also acquired from Hegel an abiding sense of the "organic relationship of subject and object, intelligence and the world," but this leading idea needed to be explicitly developed and applied to a variety of contexts. As Dewey attempted to work out for himself the consequences of the concept of organic interaction, he found Hegel and his followers less helpful than the new biology and the scientific psychology that were emerging.

While at Johns Hopkins, in addition to working with G. S. Morris, Dewey studied with G. Stanley Hall, one of the first experimental psychologists in America. Hall was deeply suspicious of what he took to be Hegelian dogma, and although he did not succeed in imparting this skepticism to Dewey when the latter was his student, he did impress upon Dewey the importance of experimental methods for a scientific understanding of psychology. Initially Dewey did not feel any conflict between his Hegelianism and his interest in experimental science. The passage we have quoted from "The New Psychology," with its distinctive Hegelian flavor, was in an article reporting the recent developments in experimental psychology. In a later article, Dewey went so far as to claim that Hegel, with his emphasis on the logic of process or experience, represented the "quintessence of the scientific spirit."[7] In his *Psychology,* published in 1887, Dewey mixed and juggled Hegelian ideas with experimental data. Hall, who reviewed the book, criticized it in the same manner in which Dewey had criticized others. Hall accused Dewey of imposing an alien philosophic dogma upon the facts of experimental science.[8]

What initially played a secondary role in Dewey's thought—the interest in experimental science and its application to biology, psychology, and the other social sciences—gradually became dominant. Although the influence of Hegel's organicism persisted, it was absorbed and transformed in Dewey's scientific perspective. The culmination of this phase of Dewey's development is reflected in an extremely important article published in 1896, "The Reflex Arc Concept in Psychology."[9] Dewey worked out in detail what was suggested in his original emphasis on organic interaction. This article became one of the classics in the development of functional psychology. But even more important, we find here the basis of Dewey's mature theory of experience as well as the starting point for his view of logic as the theory of inquiry. Because of the historical and systematic importance of this article, a careful examination of it can advance our appreciation of the direction of Dewey's thought.

The target for Dewey's criticism is the reflex arc concept, which was used by contemporary psychologists to describe and explain human behavior. According to this concept, psychic behavior can be analyzed as a mechanical sequence of three moments: sensation or peripheral stimulus, followed by idea or central process, followed by motor response. Each of these moments was thought of as a discrete event or existence, externally related to the other moments in a temporal sequence. As an example of the application of this concept Dewey cites Baldwin's analysis of reactive consciousness. Baldwin claims that there are "three elements corresponding to the three elements of the nervous arc. First, the receiving consciousness, the stimulus—say a loud, unexpected sound; second, the attention involuntarily drawn, the registering element; and, third, the muscular reaction following upon the sound—say flight from the fancied danger."[10] Or to use another example (one Dewey takes from William James' *Principles of Psychology,* a book that greatly influenced Dewey's investigations), we might interpret the behavior in which a child learns that a candle burns by saying that "the sensation of light is a stimulus to the grasping as a response, the burn resulting is a stimulus to withdrawing the hand as a response and so on."[11]

Dewey criticizes the interpretation and use of the reflex arc concept from two perspectives. In the first place, the concept is used to misdescribe what actually occurs; secondly, when used as an explanatory concept, the reflex arc concept distorts rather than explains human behavior. Using the reflex arc concept in this mechanical way ignores the prior state or "set" of the subject. "If one is reading a book, if one is hunting, if one is watching in a dark place on a lonely night, if one is performing a chemical experiment, in each case, [a] noise has a very different psychical value; it is a different experience."[12] The sound is not an independent "stimulus," for the significance of the hearing of a sound depends on a prior state and activity, or motor response. Consequently, Baldwin's illustration reverses the actual sequence of events. Furthermore, the response is not an independent event which merely follows a "stimulus." The stimulus is constitutive of the response insofar as "the sound experience must persist as a value in the running, to keep it up, to control it."[13] The response, then, is not a totally new experience, it is the original experience transformed and reconstituted. Stimulus and response are correlative, and the specific function of each is determined in relation to the other. Consequently, just as the stimulus is constitutive of the response, the response is inherent in the stimulus. For the sound is not independent of the running: it is a "running-because-of-sound."

At first glance, it might appear that Dewey is quibbling, and that he is only calling for a more detailed analysis of a complex situation. But his criticism cuts deeper, and his proposal for an organic coordination as the basic unit of behavior is a radical departure from the reflex arc concept. Dewey claims that the reflex arc concept is a survival of an older metaphysical dualism, and that it harbors all the paradoxes of how mental "stuff" and physical "stuff" interact. "Sensation is an ambiguous dweller on the border land of soul and body, the idea (or central process) is purely psychical, and the act (or movement) purely physical. Thus the reflex arc formulation is neither physical (or physiological) nor psychological; it is a mixed materialistic-spiritualistic assumption."[14] We need more than the addition of a few steps in the description of this quasi-mechanical process. We need a new way of understanding the behavioral situation where "stimulus," "central process," and "motor response" are viewed as *functions* that play a role in maintaining and reconstituting a unified coordination. The organic coordination is the fundamental unit of behavior—within this coordination, one and the same occurrence has a different function depending on the stage of development of the entire coordination.

Dewey, then, is not discrediting the distinction between stimulus and response: he wants to analyze it properly. If we think that these terms single out events that are entirely independent of each other, then the attempt to describe and explain human behavior will be hopelessly confused. Once we realize that these terms are functional, that what counts as a stimulus and what as a response depends on a changing role that the activity plays within an organic coordination, then we can better grasp what is distinctive about organic and human behavior. Another way of making the same point is to insist that the organic coordination is teleological—it is purposive behavior.[15]

When we analyze highly organized behavior such as complex instincts or well-established habits, we frequently neglect the teleological or functional character of "stimulus" and "response," because the end or goal is thoroughly organized into the means. But if we suppress the reference to an end, we can easily be misled to think of the ordered sequence as a series of discrete occurrences. Serious confusion results when the reflex arc concept is used to account for the more complex, hesitant behavior that is characteristic of thinking. The purposive, teleological, or functional character of stimulus and response cannot be ignored without distorting what takes place.

To make these various points concrete, let us examine the situation of the child who upon reaching for a light has sometimes found something good to eat and sometimes burned himself. If presented with a bright light, the child's *problem* is to discover what kind of light it is. His problem is to discover the right "stimulus." Shall he reach or not? His "response" is to determine what exactly is the "stimulus" in order to decide how the coordination is to be completed. At one stage of the coordination, the activities of reaching and withdrawing are the "stimulus" because they set the problem for the next phase of the activity. At the next moment, the act of seeing may serve as the "stimulus."

"Sensation as stimulus, is always that phase of activity requiring to be defined in order that a coordination may be completed. What the sensation will be in particular at a given time, therefore, will depend entirely upon the way in which an activity is being used. It has no fixed quality of its own."[16] Just as the stimulus is that phase of the activity that sets the problem, the response is that phase of the activity that marks the temporary solution. At one moment, fixing attention is the response because it is the act called for. At a later moment withdrawing the arm is the response. All these moments are functions within a unified experience. Summarizing his view of the organic coordination as the unit of behavior, Dewey tells us:

> The circle is a coordination, some of whose members have come in conflict with each other. It is the temporary disintegration and need of reconstitution which occasions, which affords the genesis of, the conscious distinction into sensory stimulus on one side and motor response on the other. The stimulus is that phase of the forming coordination which represents the conditions which have to be met in bringing it to a successful issue; the response is that phase of one and the same forming coordination which gives the key to meeting these conditions, which serves as instrument in effecting the successful coordination. They are therefore strictly correlative and contemporaneous.[17]

This discussion of the organic coordination ties together many of the strands in Dewey's previous philosophic investigations and points the way to his later philosophy. We now have specific reasons why Dewey objects to static, mechanical categories; they distort what actually occurs in human behavior and experience. The cosmic category of the organic, which is so prominent in Dewey's earlier Hegelian writings, is given a more restricted, naturalistic interpretation. Dewey also has explained what this concept means and how it can be used to analyze complex forms of behavior. The insights that Dewey had derived from his study of Hegel and the neo-Hegelians (although they were suggested by his first encounter with the study of physiology) are now divorced from the Hegelian context and reformulated in a terminology more congenial to an experimental, scientific temper.

At the same time, this article points the way to Dewey's later work. The idea of a conflict within a coordination or situation that demands reconstitution or reconstruction is the heart of the instrumental logic that Dewey was shortly to elaborate in detail. Even the terminology in which this instrumental logic is expressed is already present, e.g., "conflict," "problem," "reconstitution," "instrumental." Keeping in mind the original context of these terms—distinctions within an organic coordination—will help us to understand Dewey's instrumental logic and alert us against some of the more blatant misinterpretations.

Even more important, Dewey outlines a concept of experience that is central to his entire philosophy. Throughout his work, there is a criticism of the atomistic and particularistic concept of experience that has been central to traditional, especially British, empiricism. At the same time, Dewey rejects a tendency in various forms of idealism, where experience tends to become one all-encompassing whole. Experience consists of a series of interpenetrating organic coordinations. Within these coordinations we distinguish elements, but these are functional elements whose character is determined by the role they play in the process of reconstituting the coordination. The reflex arc concept is an instance of what can go wrong when we mistake distinctions that are the *result* of controlled inquiry and read them back into the *original*, concrete context from which they are abstracted.

The organic coordination Dewey proposes as a substitute for the reflex arc concept shows us how we can preserve the insights of dynamic interdependence that Hegel and his followers emphasized without being forced to the conclusion that there is only one single, organic system, in which everything is interrelated.

In 1939, looking back over the development of his philosophy, Dewey wrote that he had attempted to formulate "a *via media* between extreme atomistic pluralism and block universe monisms."[18] The concept of the organic coordination is one of the earliest formulations of this *via media*. Throughout this study of Dewey's thought, we shall follow his elaboration, refinement, and justification of this *via media*—this conception of experience as consisting of a plurality of organic coordinations.

Chapter 3

THE SHAPING OF A SOCIAL REFORMER

Throughout Dewey's intellectual development from Hegel to Darwin, one theme has been dominant: the continuity and interdependence of all phases of life. Nowhere has this been more evident than in Dewey's lifelong attempt to show the continuity between thought and action. Dewey held that authentic philosophic inquiry arises as a response to the practical conflicts of life, and he proclaimed that philosophy can and ought to be made directly relevant to the "problems of men." Dewey took seriously Plato's portrayal of the philosopher whose highest flight of speculative imagination culminates with a social and a practical turn.[1] Dewey's life exhibited the continuity between thought and action; his deepest intellectual convictions were shaped by his experience with the practical affairs of men. Until the end of his life, he sought to bring intelligence and reasonableness to bear on the most poignant social problems. Dewey even claimed that "upon the whole, the forces that have influenced me have come from persons and from situations more than from books. . . ."[2] If we are to come to understand Dewey, the man and the philosopher, then we must see how the influence of persons and situations shaped his outlook.

We can pinpoint the problem more precisely. There is little in Dewey's youth in Vermont that distinguished him from his contemporaries. His upbringing was conventional, he was religiously devout, and he seems to have accepted the values of his environment rather than rebelled against them. Yet by the end of the nineteenth century, he had become the intellectual spokesman for social reform. Lewis Feuer poses the problem succinctly when he asks, "What were these forces which helped to transform a callow Vermont boy, rooted in G.O.P. soil, Congregationalist, conventional, and devout, into the experimental philosopher of the nineties, agnostic, socialistic, and forever questioning?"[3]

The external events of Dewey's early life are unexciting. His family tradition had been one of Vermont farmers: both his parents had grown up on farms. His father left the farm to start a grocery business in Burlington. His parents were neither exceptionally rich nor poor and enjoyed the benefits of the solid middle class. The public schools that Dewey attended taught traditional subjects, and the teaching was for the most part dull and unimaginative. Even when Dewey reached high school, there was still some doubt about whether he would go on to college. During these early years, the only personality traits that distinguished Dewey from the other boys growing up in the New England town were his shyness and reticence. Though Dewey's mother embraced an evangelical, pietistic faith, and "condemned dancing, card-playing, pool, billiards, drinking, gambling and forbade her sons' doing these or [visiting] places where they were allowed,"[4] Dewey's reaction was a mild one. Not breaking with the church, he adopted a more liberal but nonetheless devout faith. Dewey's intellectual development was gradual: only during his last two years at college was there evidence of a decisive turning point in his intellectual life. Until then, there was no reason to expect that Dewey would have done anything except participate in the New England way of life that he had found so congenial. During his last years at college, he developed an interest in philosophic speculation as well as in the broader political and social issues of the day.

Despite Dewey's own disclaimer, it does seem that his original interest in philosophy and social theory was stimulated by books rather than by persons and situations. We have already referred to Dewey's encounter with T. H. Huxley's text in physiology from which he dates his original interest in philosophy. He also tells us, "In undergraduate days I had run across, in the college library, Harriet Martineau's exposition of Comte. I cannot remember that his law of 'the three stages' affected me particularly: but his idea of the disorganized character of Western modern culture, due to the disintegrative 'individualism,' and his idea of a synthesis of science that should be a regulative method of an organized social life, impressed me deeply."[5] The interest in social philosophy was further stimulated by Dewey's reading of the contemporary intellectual periodicals, especially the radical *Fortnightly Review*. Dewey came to feel more and more strongly that the excessive emphasis on individualism during the latter part of the nineteenth century was outdated and needed to be replaced by something more positive. The familiar dichotomy of the individual and society was both artificial and harmful. The quality of individuals depends on the social forms of education and cultural transmission of values, and the quality of a society depends on the extent to which it fosters the development of free creative individuals. Dewey came to believe that the only reliable way to develop a democratic society of creative individuals is by the application of scientific methods to social life.

When Dewey graduated from college, in 1879, there was still some doubt about his future. Although he decided to try his hand at high school teaching, he had difficulty getting a job. Finally in late September, several months after he graduated from the University of Vermont, he received a telegram from a cousin who was principal of a high school in Oil City, Pennsylvania, informing Dewey that there was a position open for him to teach classics, the sciences, and algebra. During his spare time, Dewey continued his reading in philosophy and wrote an article entitled "The Metaphysical Assumptions of Materialism." He decided to send it to W. T. Harris, the editor of *The Journal of Speculative Philosophy,* which was the only philosophic journal in America at that time. The letter that accompanied the manuscript reflects Dewey's uncertainty about his philosophic ability.[6]

Oil City, Pennsylvania
1 May, 1881

Editor of Journal of Speculative Philosophy
Dear Sir:

Enclosed you will find a short article on the Metaphysical Assumptions of Materialism, which I should be glad if you could make use of, in your *Review*. If you cannot, if you will be so kind as to inform me, stamps will be sent for its return.

I suppose you must be troubled with many inquiries of this sort, yet if it would not be too much to ask, I should be glad to know your opinion on it, if you make no use of it. An opinion as to whether you considered it to show ability enough of any kind to warrant my putting much of my time on that sort of subject would be thankfully received, and, as I am a young man in doubt as to how to employ my reading hours, might be of much advantage. I do not wish to ask too much of your time and attention however.

Very truly yours,
John Dewey

Harris accepted the article for publication, and we know that his reply to Dewey's inquiry was definitely encouraging. After teaching for a second year in Oil City, Dewey returned to Burlington to teach at a school in Charlotte, Vermont. He was the sole teacher in this small school. He continued his philosophic education by arranging for private tutorials with his former philosophy teacher, H. P. Torrey. Dewey was not particularly successful as a teacher in Charlotte. Besides, he was becoming more preoccupied with philosophy. With the encouragement of H. P. Torrey, he decided to apply to the new graduate school of Johns Hopkins. Once again, Dewey did not seem to stand out among his contemporaries. Although he applied for fellowship aid twice, he was not judged worthy of this aid. He nevertheless decided to borrow $500 from an aunt in order to launch a new career. Even though Dewey performed well during his first year at Johns Hopkins, when he was being considered for a teaching fellowship for his second year of graduate work, Daniel Gilman, president of Johns Hopkins, had some doubts and sought the opinion of Dewey's former teachers at Vermont. M. H. Buckham, the president of the University of Vermont and one of Dewey's former teachers, gives a very succinct portrait of what Dewey was like during his Vermont years.

Burlington, Vermont
April 3, 1883

President Gilman:
My Dear Sir:—

John Dewey has a logical, thorough-going, absolutely independent mind. He is sound and sweet all through—is true and loyal in matters of religion, and without any crotchets, or drawback of any kind, so far as I know. He is very reticent, as you see,—probably lacks a due amount of self-assertion. This is the only question that would arise in the minds of those who know him—whether he has the amount of dogmatism that a teacher ought to have. I am inclined to think that the confidence in him implied in an appointment would reinforce his own confidence in himself and go far toward overcoming this defect. . . .

Very truly yours,
M. H. BUCKHAM[7]

It is a bit ironical that Dewey, who was soon to fight all forms of dogmatism in education, should be charged with lacking the "amount of dogmatism that a teacher ought to have."

The lack of exciting external events and the gradualness of Dewey's intellectual development tell us a good deal about the man. Dewey was always modest, a bit shy, respectful of others, and developed his convictions only after a good deal of experience. The enormous influence that he exerted on others did not stem from an overwhelming personality or a glittering rhetorical ability. It was the power of his ideas, the integrity of his conviction, and the genuineness of the searching quality of his mind, that were so impressive. Only after Dewey completed his formal education and went to teach in the Midwest is there clear evidence of his involvement with the basic social changes that were taking place in America. But Dewey's character had been shaped during his Vermont years. Summing up the impact of this experience, Sidney Hook wrote the following when Dewey was eighty years old. "The Vermont and the New England of Dewey's boyhood and youth are gone. But he still carries with him the traces of its social environment, not as memories but as habits, deep preferences, and an ingrained democratic bias. They show themselves in his simplicity of manner, his basic courtesy, freedom from every variety of snobbism, and matter-of-course respect for the rights of everyone in America as a human being and a citizen."[8]

It is difficult to disentangle cause from effect in the change that was taking place in Dewey's outlook. But we can focus on three typical "experiences," which show the direction of this change: the encounter with Franklin Ford; the participation in Jane Addams' Hull House in Chicago; and the founding of the Laboratory School at the University of Chicago.

The eighties and nineties in America were a time when the disrupting social effects of the transition from a rural and agricultural society to that of a highly industrial and urban society were becoming increasingly manifest. During this time we find the growth of the union movement, which was stimulated by the excessive abuses of individualistic capitalistic development. The acuteness of social and economic conflicts, intensified by the waves of immigration, had their repercussions throughout America and gave rise to a variety of new social ideologies and movements. There were popularists, quasi-Marxists, freethinkers, free silverites, anarchists, and socialists of all varieties. Many of these movements were suffused with a quasi-religious, messianic spirit that had its roots in the evangelical tradition in America. One of the most flamboyant of those preaching a new social ideology was Franklin Ford, who had been the editor of Wall Street's *Bradstreet's*. Ford rebelled against the moneyed classes who, he claimed, were stifling the "truth." It is difficult to find coherence in the program he advocated, but he envisioned a blueprint of a social revolution led by a vanguard of the "intelligence trust." His weapon for socializing intelligence in the new industrial order would be the written word, and he conceived of a socialist-oriented newspaper that would spread the new gospel. Its editor was to be John Dewey of the philosophy department of the University of Michigan.

Ford's writings today strike us as an odd mixture of grand slogans and evangelical zeal. But he played a role in Dewey's life similar to the role that Feuerbach played for Marx. As Feuerbach provided the occasion for Marx's break with Hegel, or at least pointed Marx in the direction of the practical meaning of Hegel's idealism, this is what Ford did for Dewey. In a letter written to William James on June 3, 1891, enthusiastically recommending Ford's writings, Dewey says:

> What I got out of it is, first, the perception that the true or practical bearing of idealism—that philosophy has been the assertion of the unity of

intelligence and the external world *in idea* or subjectively, while if true in idea it must finally secure the conditions of its objective expression. And secondly, I believe that a tremendous movement is impending, when the intellectual forces which have been gathering since the Renaissance and the Reformation, shall demand complete free movement, and, by getting their physical leverage in the telegraph and printing press, shall through free inquiry in a centralized way, demand the authority of all other so-called authorities.[9]

The language of this letter is still that of the young philosophic idealist, but Dewey's concern with making philosophy "practical" is quite clear. This concern came out even more sharply when he was publicly ridiculed by the press for the newspaper, *Thought News,* that he was supposed to edit. Though the local Michigan newspapers made fun of his project, Dewey answered his critics with his typical good-natured seriousness. He declared that he wasn't planning a revolution and that he did not intend to storm the citadel of journalism:

. . . Thought News hasn't such ambitious designs. . . . Its object is not to introduce a new idea into journalism at large, but to show that philosophy has some use. You know Mr. Huxley once called philosophy a matter of lunar politics—it was all remote and abstract. That's about the way it strikes the student, and the difficulty is to show him that there is some fact to which philosophic ideas refer. That fact is the social organism. When philosophic ideas are not inculcated by themselves but used as tools to point out the meaning of phases of social life they begin to have some life and value. Instead of trying to change the newspaper business by introducing philosophy into it, the idea is to transform philosophy somewhat by introducing a little newspaper business into it. When it can be seen, for example, that Walt Whitman's poetry, the great development of short stories at present, the centralizing tendency in the railroads and the introduction of business methods into charity organizations are all parts of one organic social movement, then the philosophic ideas about organism begin to look like something definite. The facts themselves get more meaning, too, when viewed with relation to one principle than when treated separately as a jumble. . . .

Besides this, there are lots of people around the country who are scientifically interested in the study of social questions. . . . The idea is that some, at least, of this enthusiasm and social interest might be advanced from a study of the past to a study of the present. These students might investigate questions at first hand, in their own towns—questions like charity organization, the use made of psychology in the schools, an inventory of the social resources in village life, etc. Then we would have an exchange. Here at the University we are more or less shut off in our study of psychology and ethics from the facts themselves. We would get their facts and the outside inquirers would get our theory and methods. . . .[10]

So much of what was typical of Dewey is suggested in this passage. The folksy style—even though this was a newspaper interview—became dominant even in his most abstruse philosophic writing. The earnest desire to make philosophy relevant to the mundane and diverse concerns of men; the need to break out of the narrow confines of the university environment and to interact with the larger social environment of the common man; the profound conviction that the interaction of social philosophy with common man was a two-way process from which both would benefit, are all exhibited here. The statement reflects Dewey's growing dissatisfaction with philosophic speculation divorced from the affairs of men, and his growing desire to make philosophy practical. It also tells us what Dewey meant by "practical." The term "practical" is often taken to mean useful in the "bread and butter" sense, i.e., as a means to some materialistic end. This sense of the "practical" has little to do with what Dewey means. On the contrary, he was always critical of this materialistic emphasis on the practical. Dewey's emphasis on the "practical" is in the tradition of Aristotle, where the term is used to refer to the arts of doing and making, including ethics, politics, and poetics—arts concerned with the varieties of individual and social action. In seeking to make philosophy practical, Dewey intended to show how philosophy could aid in making all varieties of action more intelligent and reasonable.

Dewey's newspaper, *Thought News,* was never published, but the entire experience evidences his concern to establish the practical social significance of philosophy and stimulated him to re-examine his political and social convictions. During the years at the University of Michigan, he became more deeply involved in the social changes that were taking place around him. When he wrote on ethics, instead of using the usual textbook examples of philosophers that have little to do with real life situations, he emphasized the social and ethical problems that men actually face. Dewey is probably the first philosopher to use the example of a union strike in a philosophic discussion of ethics.

> Let us take, then, a specific case: Here is a streetcar conductor, and the question is whether he should (ought to) join in a strike which his Union has declared. I do not intend to make and resolve some hypothetical case, but simply, in order to get out of that undoubtedly adorable, yet somewhat vague, realm to which we so naturally incline when we discuss obligation, call up the kind of fact which constitutes obligation. The man thinks of his special work, with its hardships, indeed, and yet a work, an activity, and thus a form of freedom or satisfaction; he thinks of his wage, of what it buys; of his needs, his clothing, his food, his beer and pipe. He thinks of his family, and of his relations to them; his need of protecting and helping them on; his children, that he would educate, and give an evener start in the world than he had himself; he thinks of the families of his fellows; of the need that they should live decently and advance somewhat; he thinks of his bonds to his Union; he calls up the way in which families of the corporation which employs him live; he tries to realize the actual state of business, and imagine a possible failure and its consequences, and so on. Nowhere in this case do we get beyond concrete facts, and what is the "ought" but the outcome of these facts, varying as the facts vary, and expressing simply and only the situation which the facts form, so far as our

man has the intelligence to get at it? And how does this differ from any case of moral action?[11]

There is more passion in this passage than clarity. While pointing to concrete life situations, Dewey seems to get lost in the "abstractness" of the concrete. We read along nodding our heads in agreement until we realize that Dewey is skirting many of the most difficult questions. We can grant everything he says, but we want to know how are we—or the streetcar conductor—to think about all these complex relations. How are we to evaluate their significance? Dewey uses this example to show how obligation arises in concrete situations and how decisions about what we ought to do emerge from concrete facts. But what is the relation of our obligations to these facts?

Temperamentally and philosophically, Dewey was not a revolutionary but a reformer. He was skeptical of grand solutions and panaceas for social problems; he did not believe in the coming of some type of utopia. During his years at Michigan, Dewey's thought was taking a more practical turn, and he increasingly participated in various social activities, including the guidance of public education, but the means and end of the social reform were not yet clearly in focus. It was also at Ann Arbor that Dewey met G. H. Mead, who joined Dewey at the University of Chicago. Over the years, the close association of Mead and Dewey resulted in a mutual philosophic influence.

By the time Dewey moved to the University of Chicago in 1894, his commitment to direct involvement with social affairs was already solidified. The challenges and opportunities in Chicago provided an ideal environment for the merging of his philosophic interests with specific practical issues. For the first time in his life, Dewey had a chance to witness and participate for an extended period in the new urban society that was rapidly developing in America.

Chicago in the nineties was a microcosm of the economic and social changes that were taking place during the rapid development of an industrial society, and that were intensified by the influx of diverse immigrant populations. Chicago in the nineties was worlds apart from the Burlington where Dewey had grown up. Through the contact with Jane Addams' Hull House and the motley group of workers and radicals that Dewey met there, and through the founding of the Laboratory School at the University of Chicago, Dewey's social philosophy was articulated into a program of practical reform—one that had as its end-in-view the fostering of an industrial democratic community.

Hull House was founded in 1889 as a settlement house for social work among immigrant workingmen. It was the hub of radical thought and activity in Chicago. It was an "academy" for the workingman, a place where contemporary social issues were hotly debated, for struggling unions to meet and organize, and most important a place for making deep and lasting friendships based on the common commitment to practical social reform. Dewey had a chance to meet workers, to witness their daily problems, and to thrash out his ideas with radicals of all varieties. Dewey wrote of Jane Addams, who was the leader of this circle, that she "had a deep feeling that the simple, the 'humble' peoples of the earth are those in whom primitive impulses of friendly affection are the least spoiled, the most spontaneous. Her faith in democracy was indissolubly associated with this belief."[12] At Hull House, Dewey also met Florence Kelley, who was in touch with the socialist movements in Europe and who translated Engels' *The Condition of the Working-class in England in 1844,* agitated for new labor legislation in Chicago, and became the first labor inspector under the enlightened administration of Governor John P. Altgeld. Dewey met Henry Demarest Lloyd, whose *Wealth Against Commonwealth,* an exposé of the Standard Oil Company, was one of the most influential books in the muckraking movement. Dewey, one of the trustees of Hull House, also lectured to the Working-People's Social Science Club.

In short, Dewey's contact with Hull House provided him with the "facts" that he had spoken about in his defense of *Thought News.* No longer was the philosopher "shut off . . . from the facts themselves." Dewey was welcomed by the Jane Addams circle because he could bring the theory and methods of social philosophy to bear on the concrete facts. This was the very "exchange" that Dewey hoped to realize. Under the impact of the experiences at Hull House, Dewey's social philosophy became articulated and more specific. From the nineties on, he became America's intellectual spokesman for practical social reform, for the elimination of specific injustices, and for the positive reconstruction of a democratic community that would become more humane and in which all would share the benefits.

Dewey was no sentimentalist who looked back to the "golden era" of a democratic community that had its roots in a rural society. New conditions demanded new ideas. The central problem was one of finding new ways in which a democratic community of creative individuals could be encouraged in a highly developed industrial society.

Long before many others perceived the danger, Dewey realized that an unplanned development of a mass technological society could undermine the virtues of individual creativity, initiative, participation and cooperation required for the functioning of a healthy democratic community. Something had to be done to counter this tendency. And it was becoming increasingly evident that the most effective medium for social reconstruction was education through the schools.

One of the major reasons for Dewey's move to Chicago in 1894 was the opportunity to be Chairman of the Department of Philosophy, Psychology, and Pedagogy. In one department, the interests that had become dominant for Dewey were unified. Shortly after Dewey's arrival in Chicago, he helped to found an experimental elementary school, which was run under his guidance and inspiration. The concern with education—especially the education of the young—was a natural outgrowth of all Dewey's previous experience, and it served to unify his many interests. Now he had an opportunity to make philosophy practical—to bring it to bear on the varieties of human action. Indeed, at a later date, Dewey suggested that "philosophizing should focus about education as the supreme human interest in which, moreover, other problems, cosmological, moral, logical, come to a head."[13] The founding of the Laboratory School, which was commonly known as the Dewey School, fulfilled another of Dewey's aspirations. Increasingly, he saw the need to apply the methods of the sciences to the study of human phenomena. The Laboratory School was conceived in the spirit of experimentation as a place where one could test hypotheses and learn more about the psychology of the child. From this time on, Dewey's own psychological discussions became much more empirical.

As Dewey well knew, experimentation is not to be confused with random groping: it is a form of *directed* activity. The Laboratory School provided an opportunity to test and refine the ideas about human nature that had been evolving in his various investigations. In the article on the reflex arc concept, Dewey sketched a new way of viewing human behavior as consisting of active coordinations in which conflicts arise that necessitate reconstruction. This idea was now put to test in the school situation. The child, who is a naturally curious and active creature, was to be educated in such a way as to take advantage of this exploratory activity. The teacher was to guide this activity, so that the child's experience became funded with the information and skills for dealing with new problems in a more intelligent way.

It is well known that Dewey attacked what he called the "old education," which treated the child as an essentially passive creature upon whom the teacher imposed information and facts. It is commonly thought that Dewey advocated a child-centered education. Something like the following has come to be accepted as the core of Dewey's concept of the child:

> The child is the starting-point, the center, and the end. His development, his growth, is the ideal. It alone furnishes the standard. To the growth of the child all studies are subservient; they are instruments valued as they serve the needs of growth. . . . Literally, we must take our stand with the child and our departure from him. It is he and not the subject-matter which determines both quality and quantity of learning.[14]

This is a quotation from lectures that Dewey gave while in charge of the Laboratory School. But this does *not* represent his view: it represents a view that he *devastatingly criticizes*. Such a view shows a "sentimental idealization of the child's naïve caprices and performances."[15] Dewey clearly affirms that the " 'new education' is in danger of taking the idea of development in altogether too formal and empty a way."[16] He goes on to tell us:

> The child is expected to "develop" this or that fact or truth out of his own mind. He is told to think things out, or work things out for himself, without being supplied any of the environing conditions which are requisite to start and guide thought. Nothing can be developed from nothing; nothing but the crude can be developed out of the crude—and this is what surely happens when we throw the child back upon his achieved self as a finality, and invite him to spin new truths of nature or of conduct out of that.[17]

Dewey, in theory and practice, rejected the extremes of the "old" and "new" education. Both contained elements of truth, but both could have disastrous consequences when frozen into fixed dogmas. Both extremes suffered from the same common fallacy, i.e., "taking stages of growth or movement as something cut off and fixed."[18] The experience of the Laboratory School helped Dewey to formulate his conception of education as a continuing process of reconstruction in which the function of the teacher is to help provide, through the child's environment, the stimuli and cues that would lead him from his immediate fund of crude experience to more controlled, orderly, and esthetically satisfactory experience.

Throughout Dewey's philosophical, psychological, and educational interests, which found their direct expression in the Laboratory School, there is a dominant social concern. One of Dewey's early books on education, based on lectures given in connection with the Laboratory School, is entitled *The School and Society,* but it might have been more appropriately called *The School as Society,* for the social significance of the school is perhaps the most distinctive feature of the concept of education that Dewey was developing. "A society is a number of people held together because they are working along common lines, in a common spirit, and with reference to common aims. The common needs and aims demand a growing interchange of thought and growing unity of sympathetic feeling."[19] The school could function as a miniature "new society where cooperation rather than competition should rule."[20] Dewey never advocated passive adjustment to the *status quo.* On the contrary, the social character of the school becomes the most effective means for educating individuals who can correct abuses and injustices of the larger society in which they will grow up. The school becomes the most effective means for improving and reforming society. Within the school as society, the child would directly experience and develop the intellectual and moral virtues to enable him to develop a better society. Dewey's interest in social reform, originally unfocused and more passionate than persuasive, is now clearly directed to the education of the young.

In Dewey's famous *My Pedagogic Creed,* written in 1897 as a manifesto for all teachers, he fervently expresses this ideal when he declares:

I Believe that

—education is the fundamental method of social progress and reform. . . .

—education is the regulation of the process of coming to share in the social consciousness; and that the adjustment of individual activity on the basis of this social consciousness is the only sure method of social reconstruction.

—this conception has due regard for both individualistic and socialistic ideals. It is duly individualistic because it recognizes the formation of certain character as the only genuine basis of right living. It is socialistic because it recognizes that this right character is not to be formed by merely individual precept, example, or exhortation, but rather by the influence of a certain form of institutional or community life upon the individual. . . .

—it is the business of every one interested in education to insist upon the school as the primary and most effective instrument of social progress and reform in order that society may be awakened to realize what the school stands for. . . .[21]

The same motif is sounded when Dewey wrote, "When the school introduces and trains each child of society into membership within such a little community, saturating him with the spirit of service, and providing him with the instruments of effective self-direction, we shall have the deepest and best guaranty of a larger society which is worthy, lovely, and harmonious."[22]

Dewey now had found the proper medium—the

education of the young—for the center of his philosophical, psychological, scientific, and social interests. At the turn of the century, he clearly expressed his faith in the school as the most effective means for social progress and for developing the virtues required for a creative, democratic community. To the end of his life, Dewey was America's boldest defender of this faith.

Chapter 4

EXPERIENCE: THE PHILOSOPHICAL PERSPECTIVE

Dewey's distinctive genius is revealed in his ability to concentrate on specific problems and at the same time to view these in the larger intellectual and philosophic perspective of the Western tradition. As in the modern film, he could, with equal mastery, focus on a very small detail of the intellectual scene as well as move back and capture the entire panorama. Throughout the preceding chapters the concept of experience has been in the foreground. The meaning of "experience" is essential for understanding Dewey's view of philosophy as criticism—a criticism of criticisms. The intellectual development from Hegel to Darwin centers in the articulation of a new concept of experience which culminates in the analysis of the organic coordination. And it is obvious that Dewey's reflections on experience are further developed and applied in his concern with social reform, especially as it is expressed in the educational process. Dewey's philosophy represents a new empiricism, based on the theory of experience that he was evolving. By turning now to what Dewey himself took to be the strengths and weaknesses, the insights and limitations of traditional concepts of experience, we can provide the panoramic philosophic perspective for appreciating his own reconstruction.

In an essay titled "An Empirical Survey of Empiricisms,"[1] Dewey put into practice his conviction that the great philosophic systems of the past can best be evaluated in relation to the background of their cultural contexts. He isolates three main concepts of experience that have been influential in shaping philosophic thought. The first is a view that had its origins in classical Greek thought and persisted, according to Dewey, in various forms until the seventeenth century; the second is characteristic of eighteenth and early nineteenth century British empiricism, and is frequently thought of as *the* philosophic view of experience; the third has its origins in the nineteenth century, and is still in the process of development.

We find an analogue to what the Greeks meant by "experience" in our own use of the term when we speak of an experienced mechanic or craftsman. The craftsman has a practical knowledge or know-how that is based on the funded results of past encounters, and that is fairly dependable for practical purposes. The experienced craftsman is distinguished from the novice, who lacks sufficient experience, as well as from the theoretician, who lacks practical know-how. Experience "denotes the accumulated information of the past, not merely the individual's own past but the social past, transmitted through language and even more through apprenticeship in various crafts, so far as this information was condensed in matter-of-fact generalizations about how to do certain things like building a house, making a statue, leading an army, or knowing what to expect under given circumstances."[2]

In Plato, this type of practical knowledge would most closely correspond to what he calls "right opinion," and is contrasted with the highest form of knowledge, which involves a grasp of eternal reality. Dewey suggests that beginning with Plato, "experience" gets a depreciatory meaning that has clung to it throughout the classic strain in philosophy. Experience, as funded empirical information and skills based on custom and habit, is sharply distinguished from true knowledge, or science, which is based on a rational insight into the eternal nature of things.

With Aristotle we have a more localized account of experience as a stage in the hierarchy of functions, a hierarchy that begins with sense perception and culminates with the grasp of primary premises by intellectual intuition. In his typically systematic fashion, Aristotle informs us:

> All animals . . . possess a congenital discriminative capacity which is called sense-perception. But though sense-perception is innate in all animals, in some the sense-impression comes to persist, in others it does not. So animals in which this persistence does not come to be have either no knowledge at all outside the act of perceiving, or no knowledge of objects of which no impression persists; animals in which it does come into being have perception and can continue to retain the sense-impression in the soul: and when such persistence is frequently repeated a further distinction at once arises between those which out of the persistence of such sense-impressions develop a power of systematiz-

> ing them and those which do not. So out of sense-perception comes to be what we call memory, and out of frequently repeated memories of the same thing develops experience. From experience again—i.e., from the universal now stabilized in its entirety within the soul, the one beside the many which is a single identity within them all—originate the skill of the craftsman and the knowledge of the man of science. . . .[3]

Aristotle's biological-logical ordering of functions serves a double purpose: it enables us to distinguish and classify different types of animals according to the distinctive functions that they can perform; and it enables us to see the order of dependence of the various cognitive functions of animals. Experience arises only in animals capable of sense perception, memory, imagination, and systematizing memories into a single experience. But the type of knowledge that the level of experience defines is not to be confused with scientific knowledge, or with the intellectual grasp of primary premises that is the basis for scientific knowledge. "We suppose ourselves to possess unqualified scientific knowledge of a thing . . . when we think we know the cause on which the fact depends, as the cause of that fact and no other, and, further, that the fact could not be other than it is."[4] Although experience, as characterized above, is a necessary stage in coming to possess scientific knowledge, it is not sufficient to provide us with this knowledge or with the knowledge of the primary premises that serve as the foundation for scientific demonstration.

Dewey also points out that the Greek philosophers did not make the sharp dichotomy between man as a knower and man as a doer that has been characteristic of a good deal of modern philosophy. There is a continuity between thought and action such that the level and quality of action is dependent on the corresponding level of knowledge attained. But even here there is a tendency in Greek philosophy to contrast the type of practical activity that corresponds to experience with the highest form of activity—the pure activity of the pure intellect. However important experience may be as a steppingstone toward the exercise of the pure intellect, experience by itself is limited to the changing and the contingent—experience cannot reveal the nature of ultimate reality.

Dewey indicates three related limitations to this classical view of experience. There is an epistemological limitation because empirical knowledge is contrasted with the "higher" type of knowledge gained by pure reason, or nous. There is a moral limitation because "there is a restricted and dependent nature of practice in contrast with the free character of rational thought."[5] And finally, underlying these two limitations, there is a metaphysical limitation because "sense and bodily action are confined to the realm of phenomena while reason in its inherent nature is akin to ultimate reality."[6]

Dewey's approach to the Greek view of experience illustrates his general dialectical approach to the great philosophies of the past. He does not simply tell us what is wrong with the Greek view; he wants to extract the element of truth and insight in it. Indeed, he frequently thought of his own philosophy as a *critical* return to the spirit of Greek philosophy. He thought that the Greeks had profound insight into the nature of experience when they emphasized its social character and the ways in which it is developed and transmitted by habit and custom. He admired Aristotle's attempt to relate the functions by which we gain knowledge to biological functions. The Greek view of experience reflected a robust sense of man directly involved in a world of nature, and a subtle appreciation of the interplay of knowledge and action. Furthermore, the Greek account of experience was an honest report of the world that the Greeks knew: experience was distinguished from and contrasted with reason. Such a division was natural in a world where methods for making experience more rational were not yet developed. This fact, combined with the Greek discoveries in mathematics, where reason yielded a type of universal and necessary knowledge not to be found within experience, emphasized the dichotomy of experience and reason. But while a philosophy may articulate, order, and clarify existing cultural conditions, Dewey firmly believes that when the conditions change, when new methods of inquiry are developed, then the philosophic conception of experience must also change. "If the experience of the time had been the measure of all possible, all future, experience, I do not see how this conception of the nature of experience could be attacked. But the significant point to be borne in mind (one that philosophers of the present period have little excuse for ignoring) is that subsequent developments show that experience is capable of incorporating rational control within itself."[7]

The second concept of experience that Dewey isolates is that of the British empiricist tradition. He singles out Locke as a representative of this view. A dramatic reversal takes place in this tradition. Reason is no longer understood to be a pure faculty by which man can directly grasp the nature of ultimate reality.

On the contrary, many of the "truths" claimed in the name of pure reason struck Locke as disguised dogmas based on tradition and prejudice; much of what had gone under the banner of reason turned out to be irrational. There is a spirit of liberal protest that pervades Locke's epistemological and political writings. Experience now suggests something fresh and personal. Experience has its center in the individual who can test all knowledge claims and is the initiator of all action. Experience depends on direct personal contact with nature. Sensations, which are the origin and basis for our knowledge of nature, are impressed upon us by external material objects. What enables observation (whether it is observation of external material objects or the operations of the mind) to serve as an ultimate authority is its coerciveness: regardless of our prejudices, wishes, fancies and desires, something is forced upon us willy-nilly. Experience is compulsive, and can serve as the ultimate test for all beliefs.

The type of empiricism advocated by Locke was developed, refined and even drastically modified by the philosophers who followed in the empiricist tradition. With Hume, empiricism was transformed into a philosophical skepticism that called into question what Locke took as fundamental—the existence of external material objects and the personal identity of the self. Out of this empiricist tradition also arose varieties of extreme associationalism—theories of mind that claimed that mental association is the only tie that holds together the independent sensations that make up experience. In our next chapter we shall explore how and why Dewey criticized these varieties of British empiricism.

Though British empiricism is frequently studied

from an exclusively epistemological orientation, Dewey stresses the social uses of this concept of experience. As a social doctrine, British empiricism was used as an invaluable instrument of criticism for dissolving ecclesiastical and political institutions that were no longer warranted. Empiricism as a philosophy of liberal protest affirmed the inalienable rights of the individual and demanded that all institutions meet the tests of individual experience. On the positive side, sensationalist empiricism—especially as developed in France—was identified with the spirit of the Enlightenment and the belief in social progress. Once traditional institutions that had a corrupting influence on the individual were abolished, then, and only then, would the perfectibility of human nature be encouraged by means of education based on direct experience.

This empiricist concept of experience harbored many internal conflicts and contradictions, which became manifest in the course of its development. The authority of personal experience was supposed to be based on the ways in which nature impresses herself upon us, but the very existence of this external nature was seriously questioned by the skeptical and phenomenalist strains in empiricism. Though the empiricist concept of experience was developed under the impetus of the development of experimental science, paradoxically, it became increasingly difficult for empiricists to account for what is distinctive about experimental science. One, though only one, of the strains within empiricism stemmed from its emphasis on the passivity of experience. Man is viewed as a passive spectator who receives and accumulates experience. But the distinctive feature of experimentation is that it is a form of directed and regulated activity. Furthermore, traditional empiricists had difficulty in accounting for the distinctive formal features of mathematics and the ways in which mathematics is utilized in scientific theory. From Dewey's perspective, the most important characteristic of the empiricist movement was its critical, negative side. "Its power as a dissolvent of tradition and doctrine was much greater than any impetus it could give to construction. When the general cultural situation became such that a positive, constructive direction and impetus were required, there was a cultural opportunity for a new type of philosophy."[8]

As in the case of the Greek view of experience, Dewey wants to extract the "truth" ingredient in this empiricist tradition while rejecting what is false and outdated. The empiricists seized upon an important truth when they insisted that experience must be the final court of appeal for all claims to knowledge and political beliefs. Dewey was sympathetic with their rejection of any claim to knowledge of a transcendent reality. He admired their rejection and criticism of traditional prejudices and dogmas. But at the same time, he believed that they failed to develop an adequate theory of experience that would capture the spirit of experimental science. He thought that their concept of experience was not really empirical; instead of describing experience as lived or encountered, a highly abstract and artificial account of experience was forced upon the complexity of real fact.

What are the factors that have helped to create the "cultural opportunity for a new type of philosophy" that has encouraged the development of a new view of experience? Dewey isolates two factors: the rise of experimental science, and the development of a concept of psychology based on the new biological—that is, organic—orientation. Although the British empiricists paid a good deal of lip service to the importance of experimental science, their stress on tracing ideas back to ultimate origins is antithetical to the nature of experimental inquiry. Experimentation requires a free, imaginative play that goes beyond what is directly observed. Experimental science arises when hypotheses are freely imagined and then put to the test. No science would ever arise if we simply observed and recorded what we observed. Experimentation involves planned or directed activity. The issue that is uppermost in testing a scientific hypothesis is not its origins but rather its consequences. Dewey suggests that William James was one of the first philosophers to emphasize the importance of this shift. "The whole point of James's philosophy . . . is that the value of ideas is independent of their origin, that it is a matter of their outcome as they are used in directing new observation and new experiment."[9]

Dewey believed that William James also emphasized the other factor that requires the development of a new concept of experience. James's *Principles of Psychology* points the way to the development of a concept of psychology from a biological orientation. And it was James's writings that were partly responsible for the biological orientation in Dewey's own investigations. What Dewey means by a biological orientation has already been suggested in his discussion of the organic coordination as the unit of behavior. From this perspective, the priority of the subjective, the mental, and the private, which has dominated so much of modern epistemology, is not so much refuted as undermined. Sensation, perception, and thinking, viewed in the context of organic interaction, demand a new consideration of the characterization of experience.

We can now see the upshot of Dewey's discussion of the three concepts of experience. Insofar as the Greeks emphasized the social character of experience, the ways in which it is a medium for the funded information and skills of the past that are transmitted by custom and habit, they have made an important contribution to our understanding of experience. And insofar as the British empiricists have emphasized the ways in which experience must be the touchstone for evaluating social institutions and testing knowledge claims, we can still learn from them.

Both theories contain contributions to our contemporary understanding of experience. But they also contain limitations, which must now be transcended. The most serious limitation common to both theories of experience is the divorce of experience from reason. The proper contrast is no longer between experience and reason, but rather between experience that is irrational or nonrational and rational experience that is funded by intelligence. The issue has now become one of finding ways to make experience, whether it is scientific, moral, esthetic, or political experience, more reasonable and intelligent. The development and appreciation of the methods and results of experimental science and the new biological orientation of human transactions enable us to establish the effective continuity between experience and reason.

Having said this, we have only a general perspective for understanding Dewey's reconstruction of the concept of experience. We must probe deeper and examine the details of Dewey's reconstruction if we are to penetrate to the heart of his philosophy.

Chapter 5

THE RECONSTRUCTION OF EXPERIENCE

When John Dewey moved from Chicago to New York in 1904, he was already a national figure. The main outlines of his philosophy had been worked out in the *Studies in Logical Theory,* which represented the culmination of his philosophic investigations at Chicago. William James (to whom the *Studies* had been dedicated) enthusiastically greeted this work and correctly predicted that the philosophy of the "Chicago School" would dominate the American scene for the next generation. Dewey's views on the school and society were widely discussed and debated. The move to Columbia and New York stimulated a further development of Dewey's leading ideas.

At about the time Dewey moved to Columbia, Frederick J. Woodbridge, whose own distinctive variety of Aristotelian naturalism influenced Dewey, founded the *Journal of Philosophy, Psychology, and Scientific Methods.* In the first issue Woodbridge proclaimed:

> There exists no journal covering the whole field of scientific philosophy, psychology, ethics and

> logic, appearing at frequent intervals and appealing directly to the interests of all professional students. It is a matter of importance at the present time that relations between philosophy and psychology should remain intimate, and that the fundamental methods and concepts of the special sciences, now receiving attention on all sides, should be kept in touch with philosophy in its historic development.[1]

This declaration might have been written by Dewey, for it expressed his intellectual convictions. The *Journal of Philosophy* provided an excellent forum for the statement, criticism, and defense of Dewey's philosophic ideas until the end of his life. The encounter with the philosophers at Columbia who were working in different philosophic traditions provided a stimulus for sharpening his own ideas. Dewey's influence extended far beyond the professional philosophic community. It was only natural that Dewey, who headed Chicago's Department of Philosophy, Psychology, and Pedagogy, should take an active part in the life of Columbia's Teachers College. Through Teachers College, which was an international center for the instruction of teachers, Dewey's educational philosophy had its effects throughout the country and eventually throughout the world. New York, too, was the journalistic center of the country, and Dewey became a regular contributor to the leading periodicals, especially *The New Republic,* where he had an opportunity to comment on current political and social affairs, to introduce—as he had declared much earlier—"a little newspaper business into philosophy."

Both the national and the international events of the first few decades of the twentieth century deepened

Dewey's conviction that a reconstruction in philosophy was desperately needed—a reconstruction in which philosophy would become directly involved with the problems of men and point the way to a better society. Dewey reached the zenith of his popularity during the period leading up to and immediately following the First World War. The entire experience of the war shattered many older intellectual and social prejudices and traditions. In the search for new directions, Dewey's ideas had an enormous appeal for thinkers from almost every segment of society. During this period, Dewey wrote his most famous books: *Democracy and Education* (1916), *Reconstruction in Philosophy* (1920), and *Human Nature and Conduct* (1922). A passionate fervor infuses Dewey's writings, for the crisis resulting from the separation of science and morals had become acute, and the need for philosophy to overcome this dualism had become more poignant. The following passage from an essay entitled "The Need for a Recovery of Philosophy" (1917) is typical of Dewey's concern with the crises of the time and his hope for the future:

> All peoples at all times have been narrowly realistic in practice and have then employed idealization to cover up in sentiment and theory their brutalities. But never, perhaps, has the tendency been so dangerous and so tempting as with ourselves. Faith in the power of intelligence to imagine a future which is the projection of the desirable in the present, and to invent the instrumentalities of its realization, is our salvation. And it is a faith which must be nurtured and made articulate: surely a sufficiently large task for our philosophy.[2]

The essay from which this passage is taken is part of a collection of "essays in the pragmatic attitude." The publication of these essays was provoked by the publications of credos by advocates of philosophical realism and idealism—the two positions that had been most popular among American professional philosophers. Dewey wanted to show the limitations of these two positions, but at the same time he was after much bigger game. He subjected the framework of traditional philosophic problems to a radical critique. He intended to "forward the emancipation of philosophy from too intimate and exclusive attachment to traditional problems."[3] It is not the "solutions" that Dewey wanted to criticize, but the *"genuineness, under the present conditions of science and social life, of the problems."*[4]

To carry out this critique, Dewey returned to an examination of the concept of experience, and stated five contrasts between what he now collectively dubbed the "orthodox" description of experience and a view more congenial to present conditions. By commenting on each of these five contrasts, we can continue our investigation of the meaning and role of experience in Dewey's philosophy.

> *i*) In the orthodox view experience is regarded primarily as a knowledge-affair. But to the eyes not looking through ancient spectacles, it assuredly appears as an affair of the intercourse of a living being with its physical and social environment.[5]

In a good deal of traditional philosophy, even where there had been basic disagreement about the meaning of experience, a primary question had been: What kind of knowledge, if any, does experience yield? For example, although traditional empiricism and rationalism have been thought of as opposing philosophies, both philosophies have been concerned with experience as knowledge-affair—empiricists maintaining that experience is the only source of knowledge, while rationalists have argued that experience itself is never sufficient to provide genuine knowledge. Part of the basis for this disagreement stems from differing concepts of the nature of experience. Nevertheless, the investigation of experience has been epistemologically orientated. This is also true of Dewey's own early, idealistic interpretation of experience. One can detect the major shift that took place in Dewey's philosophy when he consciously rejected the interpretation of experience as primarily a knowledge-affair. There is more to experience than knowing. Furthermore, knowing, as systematic inquiry, can be properly described only when we appreciate its function within the larger context of experience. We must be careful not to distort Dewey's meaning. The question of the relation of experience to knowing and knowledge is a critical one for philosophy. Dewey's indictment is that the excessive preoccupation with experience from the perspective of the theory of knowledge has led to a distortion of the nature of experience. Philosophers have failed to give proper due to those experiential contexts in which knowing is not the primary objective.

What does it mean to insist that there is more to experience than knowing, and what is the importance of this claim? It is not difficult to grasp what Dewey intends, in fact it is quite obvious. But curiously enough, the history of philosophy is strewn with systems that have ignored the obvious. When Dewey speaks of "nonreflective" or "noncognitive" experiences, he means any type of experience in which knowing or inquiry is not the primary concern. "Anyone [who] recognizes the difference between an experiencing of quenching thirst where the perception of water is a mere incident, and an experience of water where knowledge of what water is, is the controlling interest; or between the enjoyment of social converse among friends and a study deliberately made of the character of the participants; between esthetic appreciation of a picture and an examination by a connoisseur to establish the artist"[6] recognizes the difference between noncognitive or nonreflective experiences and experiences in which knowing is primary. Dewey is not denying that there is some thinking or conscious awareness in all experiences, but only that we distort our experience as *lived* if we think that the paradigm for every experience is thinking or knowing. But what are the generic features of these experiences? In the first place, although we can distinguish an indefinite number of factors within an experience, every experience is "saturated" with some one pervasive quality. If we think of what is ordinarily called "*an* experience"—whether it is a memorable evening at the theater, a serious bout with an illness, or conducting a political campaign—we can distinguish many aspects of the experience, but there is also a pervasive quality unifying this experience that makes it "the one qualitatively unique experience which it is."[7] Recognizing the complexity of such experiences, philosophers have frequently talked as if such experiences are nothing but the aggregates of the simple "elements" that make up the experience. But such a reductive analysis can lead to a confusion between the distinctions instituted for special purposes in analyzing an experience and the experience as it is lived. All the "elements" of an experience are pervaded with a unifying quality. In chapter seven, we will examine in detail the meaning and function of immediate or pervasive quality.

A second distinguishing characteristic of experiences—whether they be primarily reflective or nonreflective—is that in every experience there is a dominant focus and an indefinite horizon or context. In every experience there is "brilliancy and obscurity, conspicuousness or apparency, and concealment or reserve, with a constant movement of redistribution."[8] At one moment of an experience one factor may dominate my attention, while in later developments this factor may pass into the background or horizon. Not only is there shifting focus within an experience, but even what stands out as most distinct and apparent has dynamic connections with other features of the experience that are not apparent, including habits and interests of the experiencer that extend backward and forward in time as well as physical features of the environment that shade indefinitely into time and space.

Even if we acknowledge the legitimacy of this way of viewing experience, the philosophic import of these claims is not yet clear. Most of our lives consist of experiences that are not primarily cognitive. We are creatures who are continually involved in doing, enjoying, suffering. When we appreciate this fact, then we can better understand the role of inquiry within the context of such overlapping and interpenetrating experiences. Inquiry arises as a response to conflicting tendencies within our experiences. Inquiry appears as "the dominant trait of a situation when there is something seriously the matter, some trouble, due to active discordance, dissentiency, conflict among factors of a prior non-intellectual experience; when . . . a situation becomes tensional."[9] The purpose of the inquiry is to locate the difficulty and to devise a method for coping with it. Precisely what is involved in the location of a "felt difficulty," in formulating it into a problem, and in devising methods for solving the problem and resolving the situation, is the subject matter of logic as the theory of inquiry. These reflections about the origin and role of inquiry have already been foreshadowed by Dewey's discussion of the organic coordination in the "Reflex Arc Concept."[10] He suggested there that inquiry arises in response to the conflicting factors within an organic coordination.

> *ii*) According to the tradition experience is (at least primarily) a psychical thing, infected throughout by "subjectivity." What experience suggests about itself is a genuinely objective world which enters into the actions and sufferings of men and undergoes modifications through their responses.[11]

This second contrast with the "tradition" is already implicit in what we have said, but it is sufficiently important to deserve special attention. Philosophy, after Descartes, took a subjectivistic turn. Descartes' dualism of mind and body, together with his conviction that the mind by itself can achieve knowledge of clear and distinct ideas, set the stage for an epistemological orientation that emphasized the primacy of mind. Experience from the side of *experiencing* became a dominant concern of philosophers. When this subjectivistic bias was followed to the bitter end, many philosophers came to believe that man is trapped in the privacy of the acts and contents of his own mind, and lacks any adequate evidence for believing that there is a world outside of his own private, subjective experience. This subjectivistic bias was fostered by an interpretation (a misinterpretation) of science. When it became apparent that the objects of scientific knowledge lack the qualities of the world as it directly appears to us, qualities such as taste, color, smells, etc., some philosophers concluded that these qualities belong exclusively to minds. Dewey claims that the line of argument leading to the conclusion that experience is exclusively mental, private, and subjective, consists of a tissue of fallacies and errors. It is of course true that there is no experience without an experienc*er* and experienc*ing*. But there is no warrant for holding that experience is *exclusively* private and subjective. It is more than a metaphor to speak of shared experience. And the most striking fact about our shared experience is the ways in which a common and objective world is enmeshed in our experience. Experience includes both the act of experiencing and what is experienced. Subjectivity is a pole, but only one pole within experience, which includes an objective dimension.

> *iii*) So far as anything beyond the bare present is recognized by established doctrine, the past exclusively counts. Registration of what has taken place, reference to precedent, is believed to be the essence of experience. Empiricism is conceived of as tied up with what has been, or is "given." But experience in its vital form is experimental, an effort to change the given; it is characterized by projection, by reaching forward into the unknown; connection with a future is its salient trait.[12]

This contrast is related to the point discussed in our exploration of Dewey's criticism of the British empiricist tradition in the previous chapter. While one might have critical reservations about the fairness of Dewey's characterization of this tradition, his positive point is clear. For it has been true that one of the dominant tendencies in traditional empiricism has been to identify experience with the results of past observations. We see this tendency in Hume's characterization of experience. He tells us:

> The nature of experience is this. We remember to have had frequent instances of the existence of one species of objects; and also remember, that the individuals of another species of objects have always attended them, and have existed in a regular order of contiguity and succession with regard to them. . . . In all those instances, from which we learn the conjunction of particular causes and effects, both the causes and effects have been perceiv'd by the senses, and are remember'd: But in all cases where we reason concerning them, there is one perceiv'd or remember'd, and the other supply'd in conformity to our past experience.[13]

Hume was concerned to explain how it is that when presented with an instance of the species of an object, we imagine the effect associated with it and believe that it will reoccur. To this extent he is concerned with the relation of past experience to the future. However, the emphasis is clearly on the role of the past and the role of memory in explicating the nature of experience. In this, the consideration of experience as the result of past encounters, Hume echoes Aristotle's view of experience. But Dewey believes that when we approach experience from a biological perspective and are sensitive to what experimental science has taught us, we will see that in instances of perception or action "anticipation is . . . more primary than recollection; projection than summoning of the past; the prospective than the retrospective."[14] Any "experience," any achieved equilibrium or adjustment is precarious. Adjustment is no timeless state: it is a continuing process, an active process in which we attempt to reshape our environment so as to eliminate ills and evils, and secure the reasonable goods and values that we want to achieve. Man is no spectator looking into a reality or nature from the outside and who simply receives and registers past perceptions. Man is an agent, an experimenter; he is essentially a future-orientated creature. Dewey's point is echoed in Stuart Hampshire's recent claim that:

> The deepest mistake in empiricist theories of perception, descending from Berkeley and Hume, has been the representation of human beings as passive observers receiving impressions from 'outside' of the mind, where the 'outside' includes our own bodies. In fact I find myself from the beginning able to act upon objects around me. In this context to act is to move at will my own body, that persisting physical thing, and thereby to bring about perceived movements of other physical things. I not only perceive my body, I also control it; I not only perceive external objects, I also manipulate them.[15]

To understand human experience, we must keep in mind that man is essentially an agent. More accurately, man is an "agent-patient" where the character of what he undergoes is affected by his activity and the character of his activity is affected by what he experiences. Dewey puts the issue succinctly when he says, "We live forward."[16]

There is a danger of misinterpreting what he is saying. There has been a shallow criticism that Dewey thinks of man as a restless actor concerned with a future that always eludes him. While it is true that life is precarious and that man is always faced with a future that is fraught with promise and hostile forces, there are genuine consummations, experiences in which there is completion and esthetic integrity in the rhythm of our lives. Furthermore, we cannot ignore the past in meeting the future. "The movement of the agent-patient to meet the future is partial and passionate; yet detached and impartial study of the past is the only alternative to luck in assuring success to passion."[17]

> *iv*) The empirical tradition is committed to particularism. Connections and continuities are supposed to be foreign to experience, to be byproducts of dubious validity. An experience that is an undergoing of an environment and a striving for its control in new directions is pregnant with connections.[18]

Dewey is here touching upon a technical point in the development of empiricism that has moral and social implications. The *tendency* toward "particularism" can be seen in Hume when he emphasizes that every perception is discrete and distinct. The precise meaning and role of this principle in Hume's philosophy is a complex issue, which has been debated by scholars.[19] It is not difficult to see what happens to the concept of experience when this principle is narrowly interpreted and carried to its logical extreme. Many empiricists have maintained that however complex experience may appear, a rigorous analysis will show that it consists of the aggregate and blending of simple, basic particulars. But then how are we to account for the continuities, connections, and relations that appear to be part of experience? Kant seized upon these limitations in empiricism and exposed the paradoxes of an extreme particularistic account of experience. He argued that if we are to understand the order and objectivity that is found in experience, then we must recognize the a priori contribution of the understanding to experience. We must recognize that there are a priori rules by which we actively organize what is "given" to us. Dewey believes that while Kant had a profound insight in recognizing the activity of thought in constituting what we know, the sharp distinctions between the a priori and the a posteriori, the analytic and the synthetic, are untenable. Kant's positive insights can be preserved without embroiling ourselves in the perplexities of how percepts and concepts can be joined together. What we need is a more "radical empiricism" that recognizes the ways in which connections, continuities, and relations are ingredients in experience, not foreign to experience or contributed to it by a special function of the understanding. This is precisely what William James attempted to show in his own variety of "radical empiricism." James was reacting against the excesses of particularism in nineteenth century sensationalistic empiricism. He argued that these so-called empiricists were superimposing a highly abstract and artificial concept of experience on the real facts. James's plea is that we should be more radical and more empirical, that we should look more carefully at our experience. When we do this, we will see the ways in which experience contains connections, continuities, and relations. Dewey was sympathetic with this reaction in James against excessive particularism, and for similar reasons: such a view is not authentically empirical.

At the same time, Dewey was suspicious of the monistic reaction to particularism. The monists went to the opposite extreme and spoke of all experience as if it were a seamless whole in which everything is ultimately unified. The monists correctly emphasized that within experience there are internal relations and continuity. They appreciated the ways in which judgment and inquiry are involved in the reconstruction of situations. But their error stems from the same source as the excessively particularistic account of experience. Both extremes seize upon a feature of experience and generalize this feature in an illegitimate manner. There is a genuine plurality of experiences that have the characteristics of integrity and fulfillment that monists have attributed to Absolute Experience, but these experiences represent the consummations of specific inquiries. The consummation of a specific inquiry "is a qualitative individual situation in which are directly incorporated and absorbed the results of the mediating processes of inquiry."[20] While the results of a given inquiry can be used in subsequent inquiries, it does not follow that every specific inquiry is a stage in the march to the Absolute where everything is systematically interrelated.

Experience consists of a series of interpenetrating situations. Although every situation has dynamic connections with other situations, every situation has a qualitatively unique character. Dewey sums up his view in a passage we have already mentioned when he says:

> . . . every experience in its direct occurrence is an interaction of environing conditions and an organism. As such it contains a fused union some*what* experienc*ed* and some processes of experienc*ing*. In its identity with a life-function, it is temporally and spatially more extensive and more internally complex than is a single thing like a stone, or a single quality like red. For no living creature could survive, save by sheer accident, if its experiences had no more reach, scope or content, than the traditional particularistic empiricism provided for. On the other hand, it is impossible to imagine a living creature coping with the entire universe at once. In other words, the theory of experiential situations which follows directly from the biological-anthropological approach is by its very nature a *via media* between extreme atomistic pluralism and block universe monisms.[21]

The moral and social implications of this *via media* are not immediately apparent. We will see them more clearly when we discuss Dewey's ethical and social theory, but we can already anticipate this discussion. The issue of whether experience does or does not contain within it connections and continuities is not merely a technical philosophical issue. If we accept the particularistic account of experience together with what the empiricists have told us about the nature of these particulars, then we are forced to the conclusion that experience is never sufficient to justify what we ought to do and how we ought to act. Experience, the slogan goes, tells us what is and what has been, not what ought to be. The justification (if any) of what we ought to do must then have some basis other than experience. This is the consequence of empiricism that set the stage for Kant's moral philosophy. Kant argued that the *justification* for moral imperatives must be based on pure reason itself, not on experience. Once again we find a cleavage between experience and reason.

Dewey claimed that this cleavage between the "is" and the "ought" that follows from the dichotomy of experience and reason has led to a severe moral crisis in which fact is separated from value, and science from moral behavior. At the core of these divisions is a faulty view of experience and reason: experience is conceived of in such a manner that it can never provide a sufficient warrant for guiding moral and social behavior. This is one more reason why the reconstruction of the concept of experience is of vital practical importance. It is certainly true that men do not discover what they ought to do by dumbly looking at what is and what has been. But Dewey argues that a *critical* examination of experience is precisely the basis for articulating and justifying our obligations and intelligently deciding what we ought to do in specific situations.

v) In the traditional notion experience and thought are antithetical terms. Inference, so far as it is other than a revival of what has been given in the past, goes beyond experience; hence it is either invalid, or else a measure of desperation by which, using experience as a springboard, we jump out to a world of stable things and other selves. But experience, taken free of the restrictions imposed by the older concept, is full of inference. There is, appar-

> ently, no conscious experience without inference; reflection is native and constant.[22]

The previous four contrasts lead up to this final, most important, contrast, which reinforces the conclusion of Dewey's survey of empiricisms discussed in the preceding chapter. Experience is not to be contrasted with thought, reason, or intelligence. Experience is "full of inference" and can be funded with intelligence. In stressing that experience is not primarily a knowledge-affair, although systematic knowing is one mode of experience, Dewey intends to highlight the role of inquiry within experience. Inquiry arises out of concrete and specific conflicts within the situations we encounter. It is the means by which we can resolve these situations through the mediation of thought. Furthermore, experience and inquiry are not limited to what is mental or private. The situations in which we are enmeshed have both subjective and objective poles, and through inquiry, we can alter the course of experience. As a living organism, man acts and reacts with an objective world. But these interactions need not be automatic and blind. "Any reaction is a venture; it involves risk. . . . But the organism's fateful intervention in the course of events is blind, its choice is random, except as it can employ what happens to it as a basis for inferring what is likely to happen later. In the degree in which it can read future results in present on-goings, its responsive choice, its partiality to this condition or that, become intelligent."[23] This leads directly to Dewey's third point, in which he emphasizes that "experience in its vital form is experimental" and is oriented toward the future. This connection with the future is the basis for intelligent activity, and it is the means by which experience can be made more rational. And it is because experience "contains" connections and continuities that we can learn from experience and evolve standards and norms for guiding future behavior from our past experience.

Dewey's exploration of the contrasts with traditional notions of experience culminates with a plea for the effective realization of intelligence in all phases of human life; not intelligence that is the "faculty of intellect honored in textbooks and neglected elsewhere,"[24] but intelligence that is "the sum-total of impulses, habits, emotions, records, and discoveries which forecast what is desirable and undesirable in future possibilities, and which contrive ingeniously in behalf of imagined good."[25] Once again, we see why Dewey's philosophy is a philosophy of education. There is no easy or wholesale way in which "creative intelligence" can be achieved. Only through the medium of carefully directed education can the habits and dispositions required for intelligent activity be firmly secured.

Chapter 6

EXPERIENCE AND NATURE

Dewey never ceased exploring and experimenting with his leading ideas. Although the outlines of his philosophic orientation were already established at the turn of the century, he returned again and again to the main themes, clarifying and testing them in new areas, meeting the challenges of his critics, exploring new directions. We have witnessed Dewey's passionate concern with "reconstruction" and the "recovery of philosophy" where the philosopher as critic would assume responsibility in helping to resolve the "problems of men." A direct concern with the practical affairs of men is characteristic of Dewey as a man and a philosopher to the very end of his life. In 1937, when Dewey was almost eighty, he was chairman of the Commission of Inquiry into the Charges Made Against Leon Trotsky in the Moscow Trials. He traveled to Mexico to interview Trotsky, and after an impartial examination of the evidence, the commission concluded that the Moscow trials were "frame-ups" and that Trotsky and his son, Sedov, were not guilty.[1] In 1941, when Bertrand Russell, who had long been Dewey's philosophic adversary, was denied permission to teach at the City

College of New York because of his views on morals, Dewey championed the cause and coedited a book protesting the case.[2] In 1949, when America was entering the infamous McCarthy era, John Dewey, who was then ninety years old, spoke out and raised doubts about the view that "no one who is known to be a member of the Communist party should be permitted to teach in any higher institution of learning."[3]

Although this direct practical concern with social problems persisted throughout his life, we can also detect a more reflective, speculative turn in Dewey's thought beginning with the publication in 1925 of the Paul Carus Lectures, *Experience and Nature.* Dewey was already past his sixty-fifth birthday. At a time when many men might have considered their life's work done, Dewey entered a new phase of his philosophic development. In addition to presenting a more systematic and careful statement of the main points of his philosophy, we discover Dewey explicitly turning his attention to metaphysics, "the descriptive study of the generic traits of existence." Dewey now introduced a distinction between philosophy as the love of wisdom and metaphysics as the cognizance of the generic traits of existence, and he sought to elaborate the metaphysics that was the basis for his philosophic views.

Whereas during the period from the 1880's until the beginning of the twentieth century, Dewey was groping toward a new experimental philosophy and moving away from his early Hegelianism, and during the first quarter of the twentieth century he was engaged in defending his views against the attacks of contemporary American critics; in the final phase of his career there was a more Olympian spirit. Dewey now carried on his philosophic dialectic with the whole tradition of Western philosophy, and was especially concerned with the ancient Greek philosophers, whom he deeply admired and with whom he felt a spiritual affinity while rejecting many of their doctrines.[4] Dewey now undertook to answer some of the most fundamental objections that had been raised against his position. He had been accused of thinking of man as a restless animal arduously striving for a goal that was always beyond reach in an indefinite future. He was charged with having an overly optimistic view of man that failed to appreciate the tragic dimension of the human situation. Most seriously, he was criticized for excessive anthropomorphism. Critics maintained that in his dominant concern with reconstructing the concept of experience, Dewey neglected the rest of reality and nature, thereby falling victim to an unwarranted anthropomorphic view of man in the world.

While Dewey's most popular books had been written during the period that centered about the First World War, his most important books—his most substantial contribution to ongoing philosophic inquiry—are *Experience and Nature* (1925), *The Quest for Certainty* (1929), *Art as Experience* (1934), and *Logic: The Theory of Inquiry* (1938). In these books, as well as in a number of important articles written during this period, we find his mature intellectual outlook systematically articulated and defended.

The very title *Experience and Nature* provides us with the essential clue for following the direction of Dewey's thought. We recall Dewey's early declaration that the "new psychology" is content to get its logic from experience, and not do violence to the sanctity and integrity of the latter, and that it "is willing to throw itself upon experience, believing that the mother which has borne it will not betray it."[5] Dewey's refusal to "betray" experience eventually led him to reject his early Hegelianism. Hegel had boldly stated in his *Phenomenology of Mind* that "the experience which consciousness has concerning itself can, by its essential principle, embrace nothing less than the entire system of consciousness, the whole realm of the truth of the mind."[6] Dewey reacted against the holism implicit in this concept of experience and its tendency to identify systematic knowledge with experience.

As Dewey declares in the introduction to his *Essays in Experimental Logic,* "The key to understanding the doctrine of these essays . . . lies in the passages regarding the temporal development of experience. Setting out from the conviction . . . that knowledge implies judgment (and hence, thinking) the essays try to show 1) that such terms as 'thinking,' 'reflection,' 'judgment' denote inquiries or the results of inquiry, and 2) that inquiry occupies an intermediate and mediating place in the development of an experience."[7] We have explored the chief characteristics of the new way of understanding experience and some of the striking differences between this new perspective and traditional concepts of experience. Dewey's concept of experience appears to be so all-inclusive that one may wonder if it is possible to distinguish experience from reality and nature. It does look as if Dewey, with his dominant concern with man in the world, has been guilty of excessive anthropomorphism.

It is precisely this misconception of his philosophy that Dewey set out to correct in *Experience and Nature.* While there is a legitimate sense in which we can speak of experience encompassing everything, there is also a legitimate and important perspective from which we can say that nature is more extensive than experience. Dewey now tells us that "experience is *of* as well as *in* nature. It is not experience which is experienced, but nature—stones, plants, animals, diseases, health, temperature, electricity, and so on. Things interacting in certain ways *are* experience; they are what is experienced. Linked in certain other ways with another natural object—the human organism—they are *how* things are experienced as well. Experience thus reaches down into nature; it has depth. It also has breadth and to an indefinitely elastic extent. It stretches. That stretch constitutes inference."[8] But it is equally true that there is more to nature than human experience. Experience is a "late comer in the history of our solar system and planet." Experience "occurs only under highly specialized conditions, such as are found in a highly organized creature which in turn requires a specialized environment." But when experience does arise in the process of evolution, "it enters into possession of some portion of nature and in such manner as to render other of its precincts accessible."[9]

It is trivially true that there can be no *knowledge* of nature until experience arises. But it certainly does not follow that we are locked up in our own experience and excluded from the rest of nature. It is by means of experience, especially scientific inquiry, that we can come to understand the distinctive features of nature and how experience is one type of natural transaction.

These preliminary remarks will become more meaningful when we better understand what Dewey means by "nature." The concept of nature is one of the oldest interests of philosophy—one could write a history of philosophy by studying the changing concepts of nature. If one were looking for a single dramatic instance of the variety of meanings of "nature" and what is at stake in the clash of these concepts, he need turn only to Shakespeare's *King Lear*. There is hardly an important scene or speech in the play where "nature" is not mentioned, and it is possible to interpret the play as a conflict between clashing concepts of nature and what is natural.

What then is Dewey's concept of nature? How is it related to what he says about experience? In asking these questions, we must keep in mind an important ambiguity. If we are interested in the specific characteristics of nature, then the only way to discover these is through systematic scientific inquiry. Dewey does not believe that the philosopher—or as he would now say, the metaphysician—has any special methods or insight into a realm of nature that transcends what we now know by scientific inquiry. It is the type of generality with which he is concerned that distinguishes the metaphysician from the practicing scientist. The metaphysician asks, What are the generic characteristics of nature? In asking this question he wants to understand the general features of the world in which scientific inquiry occurs and the ways in which this inquiry is related to other dimensions of experience and nature. Metaphysics, from this perspective, is both descriptive and hypothetical.

There are two concepts that need to be explored in order to understand what is distinctive about Dewey's view of nature. They are "transaction" and "quality." In the next chapter we shall take up the central notion of quality, and we shall examine the meaning and role of transaction in the remainder of this chapter. Thus far we have used the terms "interaction" and "transaction" interchangeably, just as Dewey did until 1946. At that time, with the help of Arthur F. Bentley, Dewey set out to define his basic philosophic terms more rigorously than he had done before.[10] Three concepts of action are now clearly distinguished, and while the terminology is new, the ideas have their roots in Dewey's earlier thought. The three concepts of action are: self-action, interaction, and transaction. Writing to a younger colleague about this attempt to restate the basic conclusions of his philosophic investigations, Dewey said that he had "started a sort of valedictory book trying to sum up as simply as it is possible for me to do my net conclusions in philosophy. It's a venture, in fact an intellectual gamble and I don't know how I'll come out. . . . The substitution of 'transaction' for 'interaction' is the nub of the whole thing."[11]

"Self-action"—the first concept of action—designates the type of action where an entity is thought to act solely under its own powers, independently of other entities. Although an entity does not act in a void, the primary function of the environment is to provide the medium through which this action is expressed. Dewey claims that this concept of action found its most notable expression in Greek philosophy and physics. In Plato's concept of the soul, the capacity for self-motion or self-action is the essential feature of the soul, and Aristotle tells us quite explicitly in his *Physics* that of those things that exist by nature (as distinguished from artifacts), "each of them has *within itself* a principle of motion."[12] Products of art such as a bed or a coat or anything of that sort "have no innate impulse to change."[13] But while such a concept of action was fundamental to Greek physics and cosmology, the concept has had a much wider significance. Such a concept of self-action has been at the heart of many ethical and political theories in which it is assumed that the source of all action lies exclusively in the individual. A social philosophy that maintains the primacy of such a view of human action will emphasize the desirability of eliminating or minimizing external constraints upon the individual. Freedom is conceived of as freedom *from* external constraints. The individual can exercise his freedom only when he is not prevented from doing so by external constraints.

The second type of action is "interaction." As this term is now used by Dewey, it has a more limited and technical meaning than it usually had in his philosophy. "Interaction" denotes the type of action that takes place among entities that are themselves permanent or relatively fixed. In this instance, we do not think of action as emanating from an entity, but rather as taking place *among* entities. This concept of action also has its roots in ancient Greek philosophy, for it is to be found already in the Greek atomists' concept of the world. Such a view received its most notable expression in Newtonian mechanics and the scientific outlook to which his mechanics gave rise. Newton tells us that "it seems probable to me that God in the beginning formed matter in solid, massy, hard, impenetrable, movable particles, of such sizes and figures, and with such other properties, in such proportion to space, as most conduced to the end for which he formed them. . . ."[14] In the beginning God created these particles and behold! he set them into motion. Even Newton's mechanics is not based on a pure interactional model, for there are vestiges of self-action in his concept of *vis inertie*. The important point to emphasize in this second concept of action is that the atoms or particles of the interaction do not themselves act. Action takes place among the atoms.

This view too can have important practical consequences when used in the formulation of a social theory. Such a view is at the basis of many varieties of mechanical determinism that claim that human freedom is an illusion. Man consists of nothing but a complex of atomistic particles in motion. If we knew the precise nature of these elements and the laws of motion, it would be possible to predict human behavior completely.

The third view of action is, now, called "transaction." It is roughly equivalent to what Dewey previously called "organic interaction." The concepts of self-action and the restricted sense of interaction presuppose that there are elements that have independent existence. There are independent individuals, which have an innate principle of motion, or there are real atoms, which interact with each other. From a transactional perspective, an "element" is a functional unit that gains its specific character from the role that it plays in the transaction. From this perspective, it is the transaction that is primary. A transaction does not occur with an aggregate or combination of elements that have an independent existence. On the contrary, what counts as an "element" is dependent on its function within a transaction. Dewey and Bentley suggest that there has been a fundamental shift of orientation in our understanding of nature—a shift that is characterized by the change from the dominance of an interactional model to that of a transactional model. This newer approach was anticipated in physics by Maxwell, when he declared in 1876:

> If we confine our attention to one of the portions of matter, we see, as it were, only one side of the transaction—namely, that which affects the portion of matter under our consideration—and we call this aspect of the phenomenon, with reference to its effect, an External force acting on that portion of matter, and with reference to its cause we call it the Action of the other portion of mat-

> ter. The opposite aspect of the stress is called the Reaction on the other portion of matter.[15]

This model for action dovetails with much of Dewey's thought. The concept of transaction echoes his interpretation of organic behavior. Dewey originally developed this concept of action under the influence of Hegel, Darwin, and a biologically oriented psychology; his claim, however, is that such a view of action is not restricted to biological phenomena but characteristic of *all* natural transactions. There are differences among different types of natural transactions, but there is also continuity in nature.

This discussion of transaction enables us to understand better what Dewey means by "nature." Nature is an "affair of affairs." Nature consists of a series of overlapping and interpenetrating transactions. We can distinguish various levels, or "plateaus," of these transactions. Each of these plateaus is at once continuous with other natural transactions and exhibits distinctive characteristics and qualities. In *Experience and Nature,* Dewey distinguishes three primary levels of natural transactions: the physico-chemical, the psycho-physical, and the level of mind or human experience.

Physico-chemical transactions are identified as those that are investigated by the physical sciences—"mass-energy" transactions. Psycho-physical transactions exhibit the same patterns of behavior characteristic of "mass-energy" transactions, but they also exhibit distinctive behavior that can distinguish them from physico-chemical transactions—a type of behavior that Dewey calls "need-demand-satisfaction" activity.

> By need is meant a condition of tensional distribution of energies such that the body is in

> a condition of uneasy or unstable equilibrium. By demand or effort is meant the fact that this state is manifested in movements which modify environing bodies in ways which react upon the body, so that its characteristic pattern of active equilibrium is restored. By satisfaction is meant the recovery of equilibrium pattern, consequent upon the changes of environment due to [transactions] with the active demands of the organism.[16]

The difference between physico-chemical and psychophysical transactions is *not* that the latter has "something in addition to physico-chemical energy; it lies in the *way* in which physico-chemical energies are interconnected and operate, whence different *consequences* mark inanimate and animate activity respectively."[17] Dewey is calling attention to a gross difference between two types of transaction. He would insist, however, that the difference is one of degree, a difference resulting from greater complexity in which there are different consequences. It is a matter of empirical science to discover the gradations between these two distinctive types of transactions. As we discover more about nature, we come to appreciate the subtle gradations in the behavior of natural transactions. At the same time, we can appreciate how Dewey's naturalism differs from traditional doctrines of materialism. He does not think that there is one type of transaction—the physico-chemical—which is the *only* real type of transaction and to which others are to be completely reduced. There are different types of transaction, which exhibit distinctive patterns of behavior and qualities, but there is no need to introduce "nonnatural" categories to account for these differences. An adequate naturalism—once again there are echoes of Aristotle—must be sensitive to both the continuities and the differences exhibited within nature.

The third distinctive level of transactions is the level of human experience or mind. Human experience does exhibit the behavior characteristic of physico-chemical transactions and psycho-physical transactions. The distinguishing feature of human experience is marked by the ability to use language. More accurately, while there are prototypes for human language in less developed animals, we can distinguish human language from animal forms of communication. With human language, feelings and sentience are discriminated and identified; feelings are "objectified." Men have the ability to manipulate signs in such a manner that a sign can be used to represent something else—something which need not be immediately present. When signs are abstracted from their immediate context and freely used to develop new signs, which can be used to explain nature, we reach the level of human experience. As a consequence of this ability to use language, the transactions characteristic of human experience are transformed and exhibit characteristics that enable us to distinguish this level of transactions from less complex transactions. Summing up this discussion, Dewey tells us:

> The distinction between physical, psycho-physical, and mental is thus one of levels of increasing complexity and intimacy of [transaction] among natural events. The idea that matter, life and mind represent separate kinds of Being is a doctrine that springs, as so many philosophic errors have sprung, from a substantiation of eventual functions. The fallacy converts consequences of [trans-

> actions] of events into causes of the occurrence of these consequences—a reduplication which is significant as to the *importance* of the functions, but which hopelessly confuses understanding of them.[18]

We can now better understand Dewey's concept of nature and why he adopted the label "naturalism" to characterize his mature philosophic position. Nature consists of a variety of transactions. We can distinguish different types or levels of transaction according to the complexity, functions and consequences of these transactions. There are no sharp breaks within nature that demand the introduction of "nonnatural" categories. For most of his life, Dewey was concerned primarily with the level of natural transactions that are exhibited in human experience, and he sought to delineate some of the major varieties of human experience. But he never would have accepted the consequence that there is nothing more to nature or reality than what is manifested at the level of human experience. Indeed, experience is *in* nature; it is one type of natural transaction embedded in a much wider range of natural transactions. Experience is *of* nature; it is a type of transaction in which the variety of other natural transactions participate.

Although this account advances our understanding of the distinctive meaning and role of "nature" for Dewey, we have not yet told the whole story. Earlier we indicated that to understand what Dewey means by nature we must explore the concept of quality. In our previous chapters, we have pointed out that one of the distinguishing characteristics of a situation or *an* experience is that it is "saturated" by a pervading quality. It is now time to explore this notion systematically. Dewey's discussion of quality is one of the most important and fascinating features of his entire philosophy.

Chapter 7

QUALITATIVE IMMEDIACY

One of the main motifs in nineteenth century thought was a quest for immediacy. In art, poetry, philosophy, and religious thought there was an increasing dissatisfaction with the "intellectualistic" emphasis in Western thought. The emphasis in the Western tradition on conceptual knowledge and abstraction had led to a neglect, and more frequently to a distortion, of the vital, dynamic, immediate, felt dimensions of life itself. There had been, as Whitehead succinctly phrased it, a "fallacy of misplaced concreteness," where abstractions important for specific purposes had been mistaken for the concrete reality from which they were abstracted. Whitehead, who played a major role in the rebellion against the traditional scientific outlook and the empiricism associated with it, concisely summed up the seventeenth century outlook that survived until the end of the nineteenth century, and which so many thinkers found disturbing:

> The primary qualities are the essential qualities of substances whose spatio-temporal relationships constitute nature. . . . The occurrences of nature are in some ways apprehended by minds which

> are associated with living bodies. . . . But the mind in apprehending also experiences sensations which, properly speaking, are qualities of the mind alone. These sensations are projected by the mind so as to clothe appropriate bodies in external nature. Thus the bodies are perceived as with qualities that do not belong to them, qualities which in fact are purely the offspring of the mind. Thus nature gets credit which in truth should be reserved for ourselves: the rose for its scent: the nightingale for his song: and the sun for his radiance. . . . Nature is a dull affair, soundless, scentless, colorless; merely the hurrying of material, endlessly, meaninglessly.[1]

Something is out of joint with this outlook, even though variations on it were accepted as the "official" scientific philosophy. What appears to be most real and valuable for man, the world that he directly encounters, suffers, and enjoys, is condemned to a nether region of the mental, the subjective, and the illusory. A new beginning was needed to avoid the logical and practical absurdities of this cleavage between nature and man's mental life. Bergson is representative of those who protested against this image of man in the world (or rather man cut off from the world), and he desperately sought for a new starting point. Beginning with a sensitive portrayal of the dynamics of psychic life, Bergson argued that the concreteness, flow, and immediacy of life eluded the "spatialized" categories of thought. He sought to reverse the thrust toward abstraction and conceptualization that he took to be the dominant characteristic of Western philosophy. Reality in its dynamic flow cannot be adequately grasped by concepts. At best, concepts give us a partial and static knowledge of reality; at worst, they falsify reality. By metaphysical intuition we can break through the limitations of our conceptual thought and grasp reality in itself. "The mind has to do violence to itself, has to reverse the direction of the operation by which it habitually thinks. . . ."[2] Metaphysics is to proceed by intuition, and by intuition Bergson means "the kind of *intellectual sympathy* by which one places oneself within an object in order to coincide with what is unique in it and consequently inexpressible."[3]

This same insistence on the living, the concrete, and immediate, and this same revolt against intellectualism, can be found in the critical writings of the English Romantic poets. While empiricism and sensationalism reigned among English philosophers, the poets proclaimed that the philosophers were blind to the depth and power of experience. The philosophers' view of experience was emasculated, and it posed a threat to the power of poetic imagination. According to the empiricist epistemology, the imagination is limited to a fancied juxtaposition and blending of discrete perceptions received by the senses and stored by the memory. The poets rebelled with a philosophic outlook of their own, which drew heavily on the insights of continental thinkers. Keats, for example, speaks of "consequitive reasoning" that categorizes and quantifies. It is the faculty par excellence of the scientist and the philosopher. But the poet, by "negative capability," must identify and unite himself with the concrete objects that he encounters. The poet is the man who can grasp, exhibit, and express what is really real.

But while nineteenth century thinkers demanded the recognition of the immediacy of experience, they frequently espoused the same fallacy that they were trying to expose. Instead of insisting that a dimension of experience and reality—qualitative immediacy—must be taken into account in a comprehensive view of man and the world, the superiority of the living and the concrete was proclaimed, and the living and the concrete were frequently identified as the really real. This, according to Dewey, represents one of the most prevalent fallacies in philosophy, viz., to mistake an important but limited feature of experience and reality and to hypostatize it into the exclusively real. This fallacy represents a confusion of metaphysics with morals. Dewey would definitely agree with Lovejoy's comment: "The demand for immediacy—for the direct and sure apprehension of what is known—has been a persistent craving among modern epistemologists—not to say the sin that doth most easily beset them."[4]

One of the most notable features of American philosophy has been the struggle to give proper due to immediacy. The theme is to be found in Peirce's claim that Firstness, the category of immediacy, is all-pervasive. It is echoed in James's emphasis on the "immediate perceptual flow" from which we carve out our concepts and to which we apply the concepts in novel ways. The theme runs through the work of Santayana in his concern with esthetic and tertiary qualities. It is found again in Whitehead's claims about the concreteness of experience and the universal presence of esthetic quality. Finally, it is the backbone of Dewey's theory of experience and nature. Dewey attempted to disentangle the important recognition of the pervasiveness of immediacy from the mistaken claim that there is immediate *knowledge*. A good slogan for Dewey's view would be: Qualitative immediacy—Yes! Immediate knowledge—No!

There are a number of respects in which Dewey's analysis of quality varies from traditional discussions.[5] First, qualities have been understood as objects of knowledge; they have been taken as the basic cognitive elements that are known by direct awareness or acquaintance. Dewey persistently argued that qualities *per se* are not directly known, if by this we mean that we have immediate, noninferential, logically indubitable knowledge of them. Qualities are not directly known, but they are directly experienced, felt, or had. The importance of this distinction between *knowing* and *having* cannot be underestimated, for Dewey, as we have seen, has emphasized that we encounter or experience the world in ways that are not primarily cognitive. To know anything we must go beyond what is immediately present, must classify and discriminate. Knowing always presupposes the employment of criteria of correct and incorrect identification and classification. Of course, we can and do know that we directly experience qualities, but this knowledge claim *about* our experience is not to be confused with the direct experiencing of a quality. Furthermore, experiencing qualities is a necessary, though not a sufficient, condition for the achievement of knowledge. Each occurrence of a quality is unique, though qualities can be classified and consequently serve as signs. For example, each occurrence of the red of a traffic light is unique, though in each instance, the occurrence of a red light can serve the same general sign function. Again, we must be careful not to confuse the direct experience of a quality with its functional use in a sign situation. Nor should we think that direct experiencing of qualities is some primitive experience that occurs at an idealized moment in the history of an individual. We have direct experiences of qualities throughout our lives.

A second major difference with traditional accounts concerns the locus of qualities. There is an oddity in speaking of the locus of a quality as being exclusively in the mind or in the external world. But this very oddity is helpful for understanding Dewey's point. Dewey argues that the claim that qualities are either exclusively mental or physical, subjective or objective, is based on a mistake. Qualities as experienced belong to a situation or context. A situation cuts across the dualism of subject and object, mental and physical. These distinctions are instituted within an inclusive context or situation. "Mental" and "physical," "subject" and "object" are not names of independent realms: they are functional distinctions instituted within situations for specific purposes. As Dewey writes, "The qualities never were 'in' the organism; they always were qualities of interactions in which both extra-organic things and organism partake . . . they are as much qualities of the things engaged as of the organism. For purposes of control they may be referred specifically to either the thing or to the organism or to a specified structure of the organism."[6] Qualities are qualities of natural transactions. A question such as, "Are qualities merely mental or physical?" is misleading. Any specific quality may be classified as either or both, depending on the specific situation and the purposes of the classification.

Third—and this is the most interesting and important difference in Dewey's analysis—qualities are not limited to those that have been classified as sense qualities, or to primary and secondary qualities. There are tertiary or pervasive qualities, which are directly felt. A situation may be cheerful, distressing, exciting, fearful, indeterminate, etc. In each instance there is a unique, pervasive quality that conditions, and is conditioned, by all the constituents of the situation. "Cheerfulness" or "fear," when used to name types of quality, do not refer exclusively to subjective feelings that are somehow locked up in an individual or projected on an indifferent external world. Dewey agrees with Peirce that "we do not define or identify quality in terms of feeling. The reverse is the case. Anything that can be called a feeling is objectively defined by reference to immediate quality: anything that is a feeling, whether of red or a noble character, or of *King Lear,* is of some immediate quality when that is present as *experience.*"[7] Or as Dewey puts the matter in his *Logic: The Theory of Inquiry*, "A situation is a whole in virtue of its immediately pervasive quality. When we describe it from the psychological side, we have to say that the situation as a qualitative whole is sensed or *felt*. . . . Stating that it is *felt* is wholly misleading if it gives the impression that the situation is a feeling or anything mentalistic. On the contrary, feeling, sensation, and emotion have themselves to be identified and described in terms of the immediate presence of a total qualitative situation."[8] The sense in which a quality can be pervasive is brought out by the following illustration. "A painting is said to have quality, or a particular painting to have a Titian or Rembrandt quality. The word thus used most certainly does not refer to any particular line, color or part of the painting. It is something that affects and modifies all the constituents of the picture and all of their relations. It is not anything that can be expressed in words for it is something that must be *had*. Discourse may, however, point out the qualities, lines, and relations by means of which pervasive and unifying quality is achieved."[9] It is not accidental that Dewey uses an example of esthetic quality in a discussion of logic. Pervasive quality *is* esthetic quality. Dewey's point is that esthetic quality is present in *any* experience that is distinctively *an* experience—one that is marked off from the rest of our experience by its wholeness, integrity, and unity.

If one asks, "Does Dewey seriously believe that there are qualities such as 'cheerfulness' that exist in the external world independently of an individual who feels cheerful?" he misses the point and subtlety of Dewey's analysis. The question presupposes the very dualism of mental and physical or internal and external which Dewey is undercutting. Any specific quality of experience is the resultant, or ending, of a transaction of organism-environment. There could not be any qualities of experience unless there were an experiencer—but, qualities do not belong exclusively to the one who experiences them.

Each of the three contrasts above helps us to better understand the role of quality in human experience. In *Experience and Nature,* however, Dewey applies the notion of qualitative immediacy to the entire realm of natural transactions. Though qualities are directly experienced or felt, qualities are endings or termini of natural transactions. "In every event there is something obdurate, self-sufficient, wholly immediate, neither a relation nor an element in a relational whole, but terminal and exclusive."[10] There are "those irreducible, infinitely plural, undefinable and indescribable qualities which a thing must *have* in order to be, and in order to be capable of becoming the subject of relations and a theme of discourse. Immediacy of existence is ineffable. But there is nothing mystical about such ineffability; it expresses the fact that of direct existence it is futile to say anything to one's self and impossible to say anything to another."[11] And in defending his views against the criticism of Santayana, Dewey says "everything which is experienced *has* immediacy, and . . . every natural existence, in its own unique and brutal particularity of existence, also *has* immediacy, so that the immediacy which characterizes things experienced is not specious."[12]

Stepping back, we see how Dewey's investigations hang together to form a comprehensive overview of man and nature. Nature consists of a variety of transactions; they are continuous and yet differ in their complexity, their consequences, and in the patterns of behavior that they exhibit. In addition to the regularities, constancies, and continuity within nature, every natural transaction *has* qualitative immediacy. There are multifarious unique qualities, which are the endings or termini of natural transactions. Experience as a variety of natural transaction is continuous with the rest of nature, and although it can be differentiated from other types of transactions, experience exhibits the generic characteristics of all natural transactions. "Qualitative individuality and constant relations, contingency and need, movement and arrest are common traits of all existence."[13] The world in which man finds himself possesses determinacy and indeterminacy. There are uniformities and "mechanism" in nature, but there are also novelties and the emergence of unexpected and unpredictable qualities. The existence of qualitative endings of transactions is the ultimate source of human value. Values in their direct occurrence are immediate qualities. "Values as such, even things having value, cannot in their *immediate existence* be reflected upon: they either are or are not; are or are not enjoyed."[14] Man is a creature who directly enjoys "goods." He has values, which occur whenever any object is welcomed and lingered over; whenever it arouses aversion and protest. It is notorious that these immediate values are evanescent and precarious and that we frequently find ourselves in situations where there are conflicting values. But man is not a mere plaything of nature, subject to her indifferent fortunes. Man does not simply await the occurrence of casual goods and the disappearance of evils. All living involves selection, choice, and decision. These can be performed indifferently, but there can also be intelligent choice.

> Possession and enjoyment of goods passes insensibly and inevitably into appraisal. First and immature experience is content simply to enjoy. But a brief course in experience enforces reflection; it requires but brief time to teach that some things sweet in the having are bitter in after-taste and in what they lead to. Primitive innocence does not last. Enjoyment ceases to be a datum and becomes a problem. As a problem, it implies intelligent inquiry into the conditions and consequences of a value-object; that is, criticism.[15]

Reflection arises from a conflict of values, and appraisal requires discrimination, evaluation, and choice. We can formulate new ends-in-view, goals to be achieved, and by understanding nature we can discover the means for realizing these goals. If we are successful in realizing these ends we achieve consummations—experiences that are funded with the results of our inquiry. These consummations are experiences marked by their harmony, integrity, and completeness. They are pervaded by a heightened esthetic quality that sets them off from other experiences. There is (or can be) a rhythm within our experience that passes from direct immediate enjoyment to critical appraisal, and from critical appraisal to consummatory experience. This general theory of nature and experience is the heart of Dewey's outlook and forms the background for properly appreciating his specific investigations of logic, ethics and social philosophy, education and democracy, art and religion.

Chapter 8

INQUIRY

In 1903, Dewey together with his students and colleagues at Chicago published a collection of essays entitled *Studies in Logical Theory* as part of the *Decennial Publications* of the University of Chicago. The work represented the culmination of Dewey's earlier investigations into logical theory, which were anticipated in "The Reflex Arc Concept in Psychology" (1896) and "Some Stages of Logical Thought" (1900). Dewey's essays from the *Studies,* together with others amplifying his ideas, were collected and reprinted in *Essays in Experimental Logic* in 1916. Although Dewey continuously returned to the study of logical theory, his most systematic treatment was presented in *Logic: The Theory of Inquiry* (1938), where he wrote, "This book is a development of ideas regarding the nature of logical theory that were first presented, some forty years ago, in *Studies in Logical Theory;* that were somewhat expanded in *Essays in Experimental Logic* and were briefly summarized with special reference to education in *How We Think.*"[1] When Dewey reached the age of ninety, he was still prepared to clarify and defend his views on the nature of logical inquiry, and he presented a "fresh statement of some of the fundamentals of my position."[2] Looking back over his investigations, he tells us, "I tried the experiment of transferring the old well-known figures from the stage of ontology to the stage of inquiry. As a consequence of this transfer, the scene as it presented itself to me was not only more coherent but definitely more instructive and humanly dramatic."[3]

The title, *Logic: The Theory of Inquiry,* succinctly tells us what Dewey means by logic and what is the subject matter of its investigations. The existence of inquiries is not a matter of doubt. In every area of life, men examine and investigate. Inquiry as a mode of conduct is accessible to objective study, and the function of logic is to discern the methods and patterns of inquiry in order to provide us with a guide for better and more successful inquiries. Logic as the theory of inquiry is therefore descriptive and prescriptive, or normative: it is descriptive insofar as it is concerned with the ways in which men actually do inquire; it is normative because its aim is to isolate, appraise and evaluate those norms and standards that are most successful in achieving warranted knowledge claims. These norms and standards are not a priori forms, nor are they externally imposed upon inquiry. Dewey's theory, "in summary form, is that all logical forms (with their characteristic properties) arise within the operation of inquiry and are concerned with control of inquiry so that it may yield warranted assertions."[4] Dewey does not mean simply that we discover logical forms when we reflect upon inquiry, but that in the course of inquiry, standards and norms are evolved, tested, and refined, and serve to guide further inquiry. There is nothing sacrosanct about these norms. While we cannot question everything in every inquiry, and must indeed presuppose guiding principles in order to engage in inquiry, these principles themselves can be refined and altered or even abandoned by the "self-corrective process of inquiry."[5]

But what precisely is inquiry? Dewey gives us the following tentative definition: "Inquiry is the controlled or directed transformation of an indeterminate situation into one that is so determinate in its constituent distinctions and relations as to convert the elements of the original situation into a unified whole."[6] This "definition" is explicated in Dewey's analysis of the various stages in the process of inquiry. By commenting on these stages, we can bring into focus the main points of his theory of inquiry.

1. *The Antecedent Conditions of Inquiry: The Indeterminate Situation.*

The definition that Dewey has given us of inquiry presupposes that we understand and appreciate the notions of experience, situation, and pervasive quality that we have been examining in the previous chapters. Inquiry is to be located and understood as it arises in response to an indeterminate situation. It is *the situation* that is indeterminate and doubtful; "*we* are doubtful because the situation is inherently doubtful."[7] The situation in which inquiry arises is indeterminate "with respect to its *issue*. If we call it *confused,* then it is meant that its outcome cannot be anticipated. It is called *obscure* when its course of movement permits of final consequences that cannot be clearly made out. It is called *conflicting* when it tends to evoke discordant responses."[8] The point to be emphasized is that inquiry arises in specific indeterminate situations, and that a situation involves a complex of factors which are united by a pervasive quality. Inquiry is not something that goes on merely in our "heads" or in our "minds" involving the manipulation of "personal states of affairs." Once again we have to rid ourselves of the dichotomies of the mental and the physical, the subjective and the objective; we must appreciate how the situation as the basic unit of experience undercuts these dualisms.

The situation that is the antecedent to inquiry is uniquely qualified by its very indeterminateness. "The peculiar quality of what pervades the given materials, constituting them a situation, is not just uncertainty at large; it is a unique doubtfulness which makes that situation to be just and only the situation it is. It is this unique quality that not only evokes the particular inquiry engaged in but that exercises control over its special procedures."[9] This last point indicates why Dewey puts so much emphasis on the *function* of pervasive quality. For when we inquire, we do not randomly grope for solutions. We have a "sense" of what is relevant and irrelevant. This is not just a careless way of speaking: "the immediate existence of quality, and of dominant and pervasive quality, is the background, the point of departure, and the regulative principle of all thinking."[10]

2. *Institution of a Problem.*

The existence of an indeterminate situation is the antecedent condition for inquiry. This situation is "precognitive": we are aware that something is wrong, troublesome, or conflicting, but we have not yet articulated the problem or problems to be confronted. "The first result of evocation of inquiry is that the situation is taken, adjudged to be problematic."[11] To discern that a situation is problematic is already an achievement; to the extent that we recognize a situation as problematic, we have moved from an immediacy, an awareness of a difficulty, to the articulation and specification of the problems to be confronted.

There are two frequent misinterpretations of Dewey that can be easily corrected here: the claim that according to Dewey we only think when we must, and that the only occasion for thinking is the occurrence of a practical difficulty. If Dewey held that man is a passive creature who waited for the occurrence of indeterminate situations, then these claims would be just. But no philosopher has emphasized more than Dewey that man is an active, experimenting creature. He does not wait for problems to arise, he can actively seek them out. The active search for genuine problems is the mark of a scientific intelligence.

> A disciplined mind takes delight in the problematic, and cherishes it until a way out is found that approves itself upon examination. The questionable becomes an active questioning, a search. . . . The scientific attitude may almost be defined as that which is capable of enjoying the doubtful; scientific method is, in one aspect, a technique for making productive use of doubt by converting it into operations of definite inquiry.[12]

Inquiry begins when we move from an indeterminate situation to the institution of a problem. This represents a transformation in the situation rather than a separate, discrete occurrence. Instituting a problem can be a very complex process. Our task is to *discover* what precisely are the problems to be investigated. As we become clearer and more articulate about the problems, we are well along in inquiry. "Problem" and "solution" are reciprocally related: what we will subsequently accept and reject as possible solutions depends on how we formulate the problems; we could also say that the closer we come to a solution the clearer we become about what is the problem.

3. *The Determination of a Problem-Solution.*

Inquiry is a progressive determination of a problem and its solution. In order to resolve the situation, we do not dumbly confront an indeterminate situation and hope for the best. We must begin to sort out the facts of the situation and entertain suggestions and hypotheses that direct us to further observation. Dewey is critical of any hard and fast distinction between observation and conceptual formulation, between fact and theory, between the perceptual and the conceptual. These distinctions are important, but they are changing, functional distinctions. In any given problematic situation, the facts of the case and what is observed must be distinguished from what is suggested and hypothetical. But there is no intrinsic mark setting off observations and facts. Not only does what is *taken* as a fact or observation vary in different types of inquiries, but, within the development of a specific inquiry, the functional status of facts and hypotheses changes in a controlled manner. Within an inquiry "perceptual and conceptual materials are instituted in functional correlativity with each other, in such manner that the former locates and describes the problem while the latter represents a possible method of solution. Both are determinations in and by inquiry of the original problematic situation whose pervasive quality controls their institution and their contents."[13]

This theme of the reciprocal, functional, and changing interdependence of observation and theory, fact and idea, percept and concept should now be familiar to us, but its importance cannot be underestimated. Many philosophers of science have emphasized the logic of proof and confirmation rather than the logic or rationale of discovery and inquiry. As a result, there has been a tendency to think of the distinctions between observation and theory, or fact and hypothesis, as hard and fast. "Observation" and "theory," or "observation language" and "theoretical language," are taken to refer to two distinct realms or languages. In the last few decades, philosophers of science have questioned and challenged these sharp dichotomies. A spirit characteristic of Dewey pervades their objections, and the functional interdependence of these distinctions has been emphasized. Instead of concentration on the logical relations of statements after inquiry has been completed, there has been a much greater attention paid to distinctions instituted in the process of scientific inquiry. Dewey's claim that when we shift our orientation to inquiry and discovery the scene is "more instructive and humanly dramatic" might well serve as a motto for the new spirit in the philosophy and history of science.[14]

4. *Reasoning.*

Reasoning—broadly speaking—is present when controlled inquiry is initiated. From the very beginning, inquiry requires sensitivity to the specific situation, selection of the relevant factors and rejection of those that are irrelevant. Imagination is required both for formulating the problems and for envisioning possible solutions. All these activities involve reasoning. However, when Dewey identifies reasoning as a specific stage in the pattern of inquiry he is using the term in a narrower sense. An idea, meaning, or hypothesis may be suggested as a possible solution. Frequently, the initial suggestion is vague and we must further understand and articulate it. "An hypothesis, once suggested and entertained, is developed in relation to other conceptual structures until it receives a form in which it can instigate and direct an experiment that will disclose precisely those conditions which have the maximum possible force in determining whether the hypothesis should be accepted or rejected."[15] Dewey is noting the importance of understanding the systematic interrelationships among our various concepts for the purposes of inquiry. Though each inquiry may be unique, the power, significance, and understanding gained in any specific inquiry depend on the ways in which the hypotheses entertained connect with other concepts and knowledge that have been achieved through inquiry. In systematic scientific inquiry, there are frequently very elaborate and complicated connections established with the rest of our conceptual structure. In this respect, too, recent investigations into the philosophy of science have underscored Dewey's point. Inquiry does not proceed by observing and generalizing from these observations. This would be hardly sufficient to provide us with theoretical understanding. In order to gain such an understanding, we must not only envision new possibilities, but we must explore their systematic interconnections with the complex network of our concepts. We must, at times, invent new hypothetical-deductive systems, which may seem to have no immediate practical connection with specific inquiries. The development of these systems and the exploration of their internal systematic connections is an essential stage for gaining theoretical understanding.

5. *The Operational Character of Facts-Meanings.*

The observed facts and the entertained ideas in an inquiry are both operational. "Ideas are operational in that they instigate and direct further operations of observation; they are proposals and plans for acting upon existing conditions to bring new facts to light and to organize all the selected facts into a coherent whole."[16] Facts too are operational. They are not merely the results of observation. They are not final and complete in themselves; nor are they sharply distinguished from ideas and hypotheses. In an inquiry there is a transaction between facts and ideas in which the character of each is transformed. Facts are operational in a variety of ways. "Some observed facts point to an idea that stands for a possible solution. This idea evokes more observations. Some of the newly observed facts link up with those previously observed and are such as to rule out other observed things with respect to their evidential function. The new order of facts suggests a modified idea (or hypothesis) which occasions new observations whose result again determines a new order of facts, and so on until the existing order is both unified and complete. In the course of this serial process, the ideas that represent possible solutions are tested or 'proved.' "[17] We do not simply collect and note "facts." If we did, we would never advance in our inquiry. Furthermore, what counts as a "fact" is dependent on the specific mode of inquiry. If we are to advance in the inquiry, if we are to make progress toward the articulation of the problems and discover their solutions, then the facts must be appropriately selected and used. Facts play a *role* in inquiry, and the role that they play changes in the development of the inquiry.

A successful inquiry results in knowledge, and knowledge can now be characterized as the warrantably assertable product of inquiry. The products may have a dual function. From the perspective of a specific inquiry, they are the objectives or *ends* of inquiry. When knowledge is achieved, the specific inquiry is completed, but in a new situation these end-products may serve as *means* for further inquiry. New discoveries and investigations may cause us to question the warrantability of these end-products. The characterization of knowledge as the warrantably assertable product of an inquiry highlights a number of the most important features of Dewey's theory of inquiry. It may be thought that Dewey has approached the "problem of knowledge" from the wrong end. His approach does reverse one of the major ways in which the problem has been attacked by traditional philosophers. One might think that we must first discover what are the distinguishing characteristics of knowledge, and then ask how this knowledge is to be achieved. What distinguishes genuine knowledge from mere fancy is the way it is related to the methods for discovering and testing it. To speak of knowledge divorced from the context of inquiry is to rip "knowledge" out of its natural context. A good deal of the sterility of traditional epistemology results from this false abstraction. There are no intrinsic features that serve to mark off genuine knowledge: it is in the context of inquiry that we find the criteria for evaluating knowledge claims.[18]

The characterization of knowledge in terms of its warranted assertability also emphasizes priority of norms and standards that are required for achieving knowledge. These norms and standards are themselves arrived at and justified through inquiry. One might think that this involves Dewey in a vicious infinite regress. We can only distinguish knowledge from fancy when we presuppose norms by which this distinction can be made. But if these norms are themselves warranted in inquiry, then this is only possible if we presuppose other norms and standards, and so on ad infinitum. While Dewey admits, and indeed insists upon, the possibility of regress, there is nothing vicious about such a regress. The very nature of inquiry is such that it is *possible* to question the legitimacy of any norm. In our dealings with the world, we gradually learn the best means for gaining and warranting knowledge. Eventually rules and methods of procedure are learned and isolated. They serve as leading principles for directing further inquiries, and they may be revised in light of the consequences of these inquiries. The regulative principles of inquiry are continually refined by further inquiry.

But it might be objected that unless our norms have some justification, we can never be absolutely certain that the end-product of any specific inquiry is *genuine* knowledge. This objection presupposes a concept of knowledge that Dewey exposes as illegitimate. Throughout the history of philosophy, the "foundation" metaphor has exerted an enormous influence on philosophers' views of what the validation of knowledge ought to be like. There has been a search for the absolute, rock-bottom foundation on which we can construct the edifice of knowledge with absolute certainty. While this paradigm does embody the important insight that in any specific inquiry there must be some fixed points from which we start and that are essential for validating knowledge claims, the foundation metaphor misleadingly suggests that there must be absolute fixed points or first principles. Dewey argues that we never have any such absolute first principles. More strongly, we never could have such first principles. Every knowledge claim, no matter how basic, is embedded in a complex network of concepts and judgments. And it is always possible to question and revise some aspect of this conceptual network. But the most important point is that it is an illusion to think that the validation of knowledge requires such an absolute foundation. Knowledge is validated in the context of inquiry, and inquiry itself is a self-corrective process. This is well illustrated in the progress of scientific knowledge. It would be absurd to say that science never yields knowledge because it is always possible that any knowledge claim can be revised or even abandoned. The possibility of such a revision is essential to scientific inquiry. This does not entail any skepticism about the possibility of knowledge. What counts as knowledge in a scientific context is precisely what can be warranted and confirmed by the leading principles of scientific inquiry. The fact that these leading principles can themselves be revised is not a reason for despair, but rather a constant challenge to develop better warranted principles and procedures of inquiry. The spirit of Dewey's concept of inquiry was summed up by a recent philosopher, who said, "For empirical knowledge, like its sophisticated extension science, is rational, not because it has a *foundation* but because it is a self-correcting enterprise which can put *any* claim in jeopardy, though not *all* at once."[19]

Chapter 9

SCIENCE AND VALUATION

In tracing the development of Dewey's thought, we have witnessed his enthusiasm for the application of scientific methods to the humane and social sciences. Dewey maintained that the main influence of Darwin upon philosophy had been to show the possibility and direction of the application of scientific method to the problems of life.

> Without the methods of Copernicus, Kepler, Galileo, and their successors in astronomy, physics, and chemistry, Darwin would have been helpless in the organic sciences. But prior to Darwin the impact of the new scientific method upon life, mind, and politics, had been arrested, because between these ideal and moral interests and the inorganic world intervened the kingdom of plants and animals. The gates of the garden of life were barred to the new ideas; and only through this garden was there access to mind and politics. The influence of Darwin upon philosophy resides in his having conquered the phenomena of life for the principle of transition, and thereby freed

> the new logic for application to mind and morals and life.[1]

Throughout his life Dewey proclaimed that the main crisis of our times resulted from the divorce of science and values. Dewey championed the application of scientific method to the entire range of human and social problems. He looked forward to the day when this application would be effectively made. He believed that the main task of philosophy in our times is to help bring about this union of science, ethics, and social philosophy. Dewey's hope and constant theme is expressed in *Reconstruction in Philosophy*.

> Until the dogma of fixed unchangeable types and species, of arrangement in classes of higher and lower, of subordination of the transitory individual to the universal or kind had been shaken in its hold upon the science of life, it was impossible that the new ideas and method should be made at home in social life and moral life. Does it not seem to be the intellectual task of the twentieth century to take this last step? When this step is taken the circle of scientific development will be rounded out and the reconstruction of philosophy made an accomplished fact.[2]

But what does this mean? How are we to apply scientific method to our social and moral life? There have been many who have believed that Dewey thought we could achieve a science of ethics which would be like any other science, such as biology or physics. Presumably such a science would consist of observations and theory where scientific laws could be discovered and confirmed in experience. To attribute such a view to Dewey is to distort what he sought to accomplish. Dewey *did* call for the application of scientific method to moral and social problems. But when we see what this concretely means, we shall see that while Dewey argued that the scientific spirit should pervade our moral and social life, he did not claim that an objective science of ethics is possible, nor did he make the mistake of thinking that "value" or "good" is the name of an empirical property that could be *discovered* by empirical science.

To appreciate the context of Dewey's discussion of value (including all values, whether they be moral, esthetic, religious, etc.), let us recall the outlines of Dewey's naturalism, especially his discussion of qualitative immediacy. In our earlier discussion, we noted that there are three senses of "end" that Dewey distinguishes: a terminus of a natural transaction; an end-in-view, which is imaginatively projected and desired; a consummation of a controlled experience. All natural transactions have their own unique, qualitative endings. In human experience these termini are the source of all direct or immediate values. The existence of these immediate values is dependent on complex transactions. Consequently, they are precarious and evanescent; they are casual endings. When there is conflict among our immediate values or desires we may be confronted with a situation in which decision and choice are demanded.

We are not, however, creatures who must wait for the fortuitous circumstances in which nature brings about the goods that we directly prize and the disappearance of the conditions that we find objectionable. We may inquire and deliberate; we may formulate ends-in-view—ends that are chosen for resolving the conflicts of specific situations and will bring into existence states of affairs that are judged desirable. These ends-in-view are, in part, determined by the norms and standards of our shared experience in the community, and, in part, by the pressing demands of the specific practical situation in which we are involved. "Wherever there is an *end-in-view* of any sort whatever, there is affective-*ideational*-motor activity; or, in terms of the dual meaning of valuation, there is union of prizing and appraising. Observation of the results obtained, of *actual* consequences in their agreement with and difference from ends anticipated or held in view, thus provides the conditions by which desires and interests (and hence valuations) are matured and tested."[3] This leads directly to the third sense of "end" —consummation. We not only suffer conflicts of our immediate values and formulate ends-in-view as well as the means for achieving these ends-in-view—we also can achieve or realize these ends-in-view. Such experiences are consummatory experiences, experiences marked by their integrity and completeness, experiences pervaded by a heightened esthetic quality. Consummations have a quality of finality, although there are no final consummations. As long as we are alive there will always be problems and conflicts, but it is important to realize that there are and can be consummations—ends-in-view that are concretely realized.

From this sketch of the three senses of "end," an important distinction or double meaning of "value" emerges. We value something when we take an interest in it, enjoy it, prize it. "To value" in this sense signifies a direct or immediate experience. One *has* values; we cherish or esteem objects, experiences, or persons. The other meaning of "to value"—valuation—signifies to judge, to appraise, to evaluate. Valuation is a deliberative process culminating in a value judgment. The difference between these two meanings of "value" is illustrated in the following example. I may enjoy going to symphonic concerts; this is the type of experience that I prize or directly value. But when I am confronted with the question of whether I ought to go to a concert tonight, this immediate value may conflict with other values or desires. A judgment of what I ought to do here and now is demanded. I must evaluate the alternative actions in order to decide what I ought to do.

The type of situation in which valuation occurs is one that is incomplete and requires some action to complete it. The judgments that result from valuation are expressed in such terms as "it is better, wiser, more prudent, right, advisable, opportune, expedient, etc., to act thus and so."[4] The judgment within such a situation is itself a factor in determining the outcome of the situation, for it directs us to some specific means for resolving the situation. But how are we to decide what we ought to do? Exactly where does the value element enter into our judgment? Value that is the result of deliberation is not something that belongs to objects inherently and is "discovered." "To judge value is to engage in instituting a determinate value where none is given."[5] Something gains value through the process of valuation. But still we ask, how does this occur? The problem recalls one that we encountered earlier in Dewey's example of deciding whether to join a union strike. We want to know what we are to look for in a situation, and how we are to appraise the various alternative actions. And we want to know in what ways does valuation resemble scientific inquiry. Dewey begins to answer these questions when he says,

> There are conflicting desires and alternative apparent goods. What is needed is to find the right course of action, the right good. Hence, inquiry is exacted; observation of the detailed makeup of the situation; analysis into its diverse factors: clarification of what is obscure; discounting of the more insistent and vivid traits; tracing consequences of the various modes of action that suggest themselves; regarding the decision reached as hypothetical and tentative until the anticipated or supposed consequences which led to its adoption have been squared with actual consequences.[6]

We must therefore examine both the conditions of the specific situation and the consequences of possible courses of action. We can still ask what is the relevance of this investigation to judging, deciding and choosing. Something vital is missing. If we watch Dewey in slow motion, I think we get an essential clue to this "missing link." Dewey wrote the following to clarify the type of situation in which valuation occurs.

> Sometimes every immediate good or intrinsic good goes back on us. We do not confront any indubitable good. We are in the dark as to what we *should* regard with passionate esteem; we are beginning to suspect that something we prized unquestioningly and directly in the past is no longer worth our while, because of some growth on our part or some change in conditions. Now in such a state of affairs we may of course trust to luck; we may wait for something to turn up which will afford a new unquestioned object to cherish and hold to. But sometimes we attempt to further by

> means of deliberation the production of such a good. We search in order to form an estimate of what would be the good of the situation if we could attain it. Add to these conditions the further condition that we cannot be *sure* that we shall prize or like the thing in question until it has been brought into existence by an act following upon a judgment, and we have before us the kind of situation with which I was concerned.[7]

If we examine this passage carefully, we see the mutual interplay of valuing as a direct immediate experience and valuation as inquiry.

When confronted with practical situations that demand action, we may deliberate about what we ought to do. In this process our direct, immediate values are transformed. Putting the matter in terms of desires, through deliberation our desires themselves are reconstructed; we form new desires. What, then, is the difference between those values that we have before deliberation and those which we have after deliberation? For Dewey, there is all the difference in the world. Here we come closer to the "missing link." The difference does not consist in the discovery of some new property or value-entity, though surely what we discover may rationally influence our decision and choice. The difference between those values that we have without reflection and deliberation and those that are chosen after deliberation is precisely that the latter are informed and enlightened by our deliberation. They are reasonable goods and reflect a reasoned choice. Although valuing as prizing is direct and immediate, it is not isolated from deliberation. On the contrary—our direct values can be funded with the results of our deliberation.

> Deliberation is actually an imaginative rehearsal of various courses of conduct. We give way, *in our mind,* to some impulse; we try, *in our mind,* some plan. Following its career through various steps, we find ourselves in imagination in the presence of the consequences that would follow: and we then like or approve, or dislike and disapprove, these consequences, we find the original impulse or plan good or bad. Deliberation is dramatic and active, not mathematical and impersonal; and hence it has the intuitive, the direct factor in it.[8]

Confronted with a practical situation in which something is to be done, and where we are not certain what we ought to do, we may deliberate in order to come to a clearer understanding of the situation and the consequences of possible courses of action. The extent and freedom of any specific deliberation is limited by the demands of the situation itself. Our decision about what to do is not something that follows "deductively" from our deliberation, but there is an intimate and rational connection between our deliberations and our decisions.

Before proceeding with our analysis, it will be helpful to become clearer about what Dewey is doing. His investigation is not intended to be an empirical report of what we do when confronted with a situation in which there is some basic conflict of values. Frequently, we attempt to escape blindly from these situations, or rely on pat formulas, instead of deliberating. Dewey examines valuation in the same spirit in which he has examined the general structure of inquiry. His aim is to discover those procedures that provide us with the most enlightened and intelligent values. There is, therefore, a critical or normative aspect of Dewey's discussion of valuation. He is not interested solely in describing the ways in which men do make and "justify" decisions and choices; he is telling us how men *ought* to engage in valuation. But his proposals or recommendations are not arbitrary; they are based on what he takes to be the most enlightened and intelligent ways in which we actually do decide, choose, and act. In this respect, Dewey reminds us of Aristotle, who thought of ethics as based on a critical appraisal of how virtuous men act.

We have reached a stage in our discussion where it is necessary to look at the larger context within which valuation occurs. If we were to express Dewey's proposal schematically, we might say, *x* is valuable in a given situation if and only if it is desired or prized after we have deliberated. But if we consider this schema in isolation, as is so often done in contemporary ethical analysis, we would be left with a distorted picture of Dewey's theory of valuation.

For it might be objected that the formula, "*x* is valuable in a given situation if and only if it is desired or prized after we have deliberated," can*not* stand by itself. Don't the criminal and the tyrant also deliberate? Don't they carefully consider the consequences of their actions in concrete situations? And surely we would not want to say that something is valuable simply because they desired it after deliberation. There must be some way of distinguishing good and bad deliberations, and then we are forced back to the problem of supplying some independent criteria for what is good and bad. Furthermore, it might be objected that there must be some criteria for distinguishing genuine deliberation from what only seems to be deliberation and may well be rationalization. And what are we to say about those situations where we must act and simply do not have time to deliberate?

These objections are basically sound. But they are not objections against Dewey's view. They help us to see the main thrust of his reflections on value and valuation.[9] Telling us that men frequently deliberate in moral situations, or even that men ought to deliberate, is not to tell us very much; we want to know how we should deliberate in order to reach an intelligent and morally sound decision. It is here that we find the distinctive features of Dewey's theory of valuation. He believed that our deliberations can be pervaded with a scientific spirit, and he believed that our deliberations can be effective if the habits, dispositions, and skills required for intelligence are fostered and developed in our social life. Men do not become intelligent or rational by willing it or by being told to do so: they must be trained to be intelligent, and this is the primary function of education. Dewey's theory of valuation leads directly to social action—developing and reconstructing those institutions that will foster the *growth* of intelligence in the life of the community.

There are no pat formulas for solving moral problems. Those who look to philosophy for a definitive guide for what decisions they ought to make in specific situations are looking for something that they will not and cannot find. Each practical situation is unique, and what is specifically judged to be valuable in the situation depends on the unique complexion of the situation. But although every situation is unique, it is similar in some respects to other situations. In every situation, we use information and employ principles that serve as guides for deliberating. These principles are hypothetical and flexible; they can be modified or abandoned on the basis of further experience. They are stable without being static. In a particular situation they may *function* as absolutes, but this means that in a given situation they are *taken* as basic and fixed, although there is always the possibility of revising them in further inquiry.

Principles, standards, guides become effective when they are embodied in the living habits and rules of the community. Moral behavior is rule-regulated behavior. Rules, which are sometimes codified into explicit laws, are part of the fabric of community life. But although habits, customs, and rules are the fabric of human and social life, they may be blind, rigid, and irrational, or they may themselves be flexible, hypothetical, and informed by rational deliberation. A good deal of modern ethical discussion has been plagued with sharp cleavages between the cognitive and the noncognitive; the descriptive and the emotive; the habitual and the rational. At the heart of these dichotomies is the narrow and illegitimate concept that reason is separate from the emotional and volitional aspects of human life. But throughout his career Dewey systematically criticized these dualisms and divisions. He sought to make us aware of a richer and broader concept of reason—or, to use his distinctive term, "intelligence." Our values, our desires, our habits, can be nonrational or even irrational, but they are not forever cut off from our intelligence. They can be informed and transformed by intelligent deliberations. And we can work toward the realization of a community in which each and every individual is encouraged to fully develop his intelligence.

Intelligence consists of keen observation, the ability to discount private prejudices in favor of a bias of objectivity, the ability to envision ideals by which we can satisfactorily resolve situations in which conflicts arise, the ability to formulate relevant hypotheses, and a willingness to revise them in light of new experiences. An intelligent person is sensitive to the practical demands of situations and knows how far to carry his deliberations. In those situations in which immediate action is demanded, the funded experience of the intelligent person guides his action.

The set of dispositions and character traits that make up intelligence must be carefully developed by practice and guidance. Intelligence is not opposed to all desires: rather, it is the means of liberating and directing desire and impulse. "What intelligence has to do in the service of impulse is to act not as its obedient servant but as its clarifier and liberator."[10] Deliberation does not consist of struggling against all desires and inclinations. When we deliberate we reject some of the things that we immediately prize and desire when we come to understand their connections and consequences, but we do this in order to formulate and achieve ends-in-view that we desire after, or, more accurately, *through* deliberation. In this way our desires and our selves are reconstructed through deliberation and action.

We can now return to the questions that we raised at the beginning of this chapter concerning the relationship of scientific inquiry to our moral and social life. Philosophy, as was said earlier, will not tell us what decisions to make; it does, however, attempt to point out how we should best go about making decisions. It should be clear that any information gained through scientific inquiry may be crucially relevant in facing specific moral and social problems. Philosophers have too frequently failed to appreciate the extent to which information gained through scientific inquiry can be *decisive* in specific moral and social situations. For example, the more we know about the consequences of exploding nuclear weapons, the more informed will be our decisions in which we risk using them.

Scientific inquiry can be even more directly relevant to our moral and social life. Dewey called for the extensive development of the humane and social sciences, not because he believed that the information gained from these sciences would by itself solve our problems. The scientific knowledge of man gained through the social sciences can play an enormous role in intelligently determining our decisions, choices and actions. There is a strain in philosophic ethics, going back to Hume and Kant, that emphasizes the distinction between what is and what ought to be. This is an important distinction insofar as it warns us against identifying what is or what has been with our norms of what ought to be. This distinction can be and has been used in misleading ways. It is sometimes used to "justify" the claim that any scientific information about man is totally irrelevant to "justifying" what ought to be. This dichotomy fails to appreciate the intimate *rational* connection between our knowledge of human nature and our decisions about what ought to be. The interplay between scientific knowledge of man and deliberations about what ought to be is exemplified in the contemporary debates concerning law and psychiatry. We do not say that what we can learn from psychiatry is irrelevant to our moral and legal concerns; this rigidified compartmentalization would surely be irrational. As we become more knowledgeable about the nature and conditions of mental illness and insanity we can design better and more adequate criminal laws. And we justify our proposed modifications and revisions of the law by appealing to what we have scientifically discovered and confirmed.

It might be objected that while it is true that information gained through scientific inquiry may be relevant to making moral and social decisions, this information does not *by itself* dictate these decisions. Dewey would certainly agree with this, but this brings us to the most interesting and important relation between scientific inquiry and our moral and social life. Scientific inquiry is not morally neutral. Scientific inquiry demands sensitivity to specific situations; fertile imagination; a willingness to test our hypotheses, submit them to public tests of confirmation, and to reject or modify hypotheses in the light of further experience. These are the very traits required for making intelligent decisions and choice. "Wide sympathy, keen sensitiveness, persistence in the face of the disagreeable, balance of interests enabling us to undertake the work of analysis and decision intelligently are the distinctively moral traits—the virtues or moral excellences."[11] In short, Dewey is recommending a norm of how we ought to deliberate. It is a norm grounded in his appreciation of the virtues required for scientific inquiry. He advocates that the same traits should be developed in connection with making moral and social decisions. This is what Dewey means when he claims that the scientific spirit can and ought to pervade our moral and social life.

It should be clear by now that Dewey's conception of science and valuation is not an isolated, compartmentalized dimension of his thought. We must understand his reflections on value and valuation against the background of his conception of nature as consisting of interpenetrating natural transactions that have their own immediate, qualitative endings. At the same time, the analysis of valuation leads directly to a consideration of Dewey's views on the democratic community and the educational process—for if a scientific spirit is to become effective in our moral and social life, this will be achieved in the shared life of the community through its educational institutions.

Chapter 10

THE COMMUNITY, THE INDIVIDUAL, AND THE EDUCATIVE PROCESS

The pragmatic philosophers rebelled against the Cartesianism that affected (one might say *in*fected) modern philosophy. In 1868, Peirce wrote a series of revolutionary articles dramatically attacking Cartesianism, which he took to be the cancer of modern philosophy.[1] In one fell swoop he sought to demolish the interrelated motifs that are involved in Cartesianism: the ontological duality of mind and body; the subjective individualism implicit in the ultimate appeal to direct personal verification; the method of universal doubt that was supposed to lead to infallible truths; the doctrine that language and signs are external disguises for thought; the doctrine that vagueness is unreal and that the philosophic endeavor is to know clearly and distinctly a completely determinate reality; and, most fundamentally, the doctrine that we can break out of our system of signs and have direct, intuitive knowledge of objects.[2] Peirce sought to work out a comprehensive philosophic outlook that challenged the Cartesian tradition at its roots—an outlook that emphasized the primacy of the "community of inquirers."

There is an intimate connection between the concepts of the community, the real and the true.

> The real, then, is that which, sooner or later, information and reasoning would finally result in, and which is therefore independent of the vagaries of me and you. Thus, the very origin of the conception of reality shows that this conception essentially involves the notion of a COMMUNITY, without definite limits, and capable of a definite increase of knowledge. And so those two series of cognition—the real and the unreal—consist of those which, at a time sufficiently future, the community will always continue to reaffirm; and those which, under the same conditions, will ever after be denied. Now a proposition whose falsity can never be discovered, and the error of which therefore is absolutely incognizable, contains, upon our principle, absolutely no error. Consequently, that which is thought in these cognitions is the real, as it really is. There is nothing, then, to prevent our knowing outward things as they really are, and it is most likely that we do thus know them in numberless cases, although we can never be absolutely certain of doing so in any special case.[3]

Although Peirce taught at Johns Hopkins when Dewey went there as a graduate student, Dewey was not directly influenced by him. Dewey was then caught up in the mysteries of Hegel. As Dewey's thought developed, he came closer and closer to the spirit of Peirce's philosophy. The emphasis on the social and the community, which is so central to Peirce's outlook and which became the cornerstone of Royce's philosophy,[4] was given still another twist in Dewey's philosophy.

Dewey's appreciation of the significance of communication and the community is clearly expressed in *Experience and Nature*:

> Of all affairs, communication is the most wonderful. That things should be able to pass from the plane of external pushing and pulling to that of revealing themselves to man, and thereby to themselves; and that the fruit of communication should be participation, sharing, is a wonder by the side of which transubstantiation pales. When communication occurs, all natural events are subject to reconsideration and revision; they are re-adapted to meet the requirements of conversation, whether it be public discourse or that preliminary discourse termed thinking.[5]

In our discussion of the "plateaus" of natural transactions, we noted that the distinguishing characteristic of human experience is the emergence of language and communication. The category of the "social" is *the* inclusive philosophic category. The social as a category indicates "the richest, fullest, and most delicately subtle" mode of natural transactions.[6] At the level of social phenomena, physico-chemical and psycho-physical transactions take on new significance. When we consider such distinctions as the "mental" and the "physical" from the perspective of the social as the inclusive philosophic category, many of the traditional problems centering on this distinction dissolve, and we open new paths of investigation. "Now of the mental as of the physical and organic it may be said that it operates as an included factor within social phenomena, since the mental is empirically discernible only where association is manifested in the form of participation and communication."[7]

Although Dewey argues that the social is a distinctive category, he maintained that this category is compatible with a robust naturalism. Social phenomena are continuous with the rest of nature. Social transactions can be distinguished from other natural transactions by the *consequences* that follow from the distinctive patterns of human association. For example, linguistic phenomena are not to be explicated as an external expression of private and mental processes, but rather by exploring the *use* made of gestures, sounds and marks. Thought is analyzed as an internal dialogue. Communication both presupposes and facilitates basic agreement and sharing; communication is based on shared experience and joint activity. Not only is there a sharing of cognitive or rational experience in communication, but also a sharing of attitudes, emotions, desires, norms, and ends-in-view. "Communication is uniquely instrumental and uniquely final. It is instrumental as liberating us from the otherwise overwhelming pressure of events and enabling us to live in a world of things that have meaning. It is final as a sharing in the objects and arts precious to a community, a sharing whereby meanings are enhanced, deepened, and solidified in the sense of communion."[8]

The idea of community, developing through the "community of inquirers" that is fundamental for Peirce and the "Great Community" that Royce envisioned as the true meaning of the Christian ideal of the kingdom of heaven, is given a distinctively practical turn in Dewey's concept of the democratic community. In his discussions of democracy, Dewey stressed the role of community life. "A democracy is more than a form of government; it is primarily a mode of associated life, of conjoint communicated experience."[9] There are two traits that Dewey isolates as characterizing a democratically constituted society: the fostering of *varied* points of shared common interest with a strong reliance upon the recognition of mutual interests in social control; and a "continuous readjustment through meeting new situations produced by varied intercourse."[10] "Democracy" has a distinctively moral sense for Dewey; it is a moral ideal. As such, it is "the belief in the ability of human experience to generate the aims and methods by which further experience will grow in ordered richness."[11]

Dewey quite frankly admits that his concept of and faith in democracy are an expression of the common American heritage. But Dewey does add something new to our understanding of democracy—the alliance of democracy with the scientific spirit.

> It is of the nature of science not so much to tolerate as to welcome diversity of opinion, while it insists that inquiry brings the evidence of observed facts to bear to effect a consensus of conclusions —and even then to hold the conclusion subject to what is ascertained and made public in further new inquiries. I would not claim that any existing democracy has ever made complete or adequate use of scientific method in deciding upon its policies. But freedom of inquiry, toleration of diverse views, freedom of communication, the distribution of what is found out to every individual as the ultimate intellectual consumer, are involved in the democratic as in the scientific method.[12]

The future of democracy "is allied with the spread of the scientific attitude."[13] Science can only function within a community in which the norms of scientific inquiry are accepted and tested by self-corrective procedures. So, too, democracy requires the acceptance of shared values that are at once stable and flexible, and not only toleration but encouragement of public criticism.

It has been objected that Dewey's emphasis on the social and the role of the community neglects the importance of the private and the individual—that Dewey, in his attempt to escape the evils of excessive subjectivism, has lost the insight that is ingredient in those philosophies that have focused on the individual.

There is no doubt that in fighting subjectivism on all fronts, Dewey did focus on the social as a category. But the charge that Dewey neglected the role of the individual is simply not true. As a recent writer on Dewey has suggested, it is possible to look at the whole of Dewey's philosophy as dominated by the viewpoint that "human self-realization [is] achieved through the interaction with nature."[14] Dewey did attack individualistic philosophies, but not because he favored the social in opposition to the individual: rather, because the times demanded a new concept of individualism. Dewey's life spanned the radical changes that were taking place in America. He perceived quite acutely that the fortuitous set of circumstances that had given birth to American democracy were rapidly disappearing. The "ways of life and institutions which were once the natural, almost the inevitable, products of fortunate conditions have now to be won by conscious and resolute effort."[15] The very agencies that were originally looked upon as those that would advance the cause of democratic freedom now pose the most serious threats to democracy. The spread of literacy, the effectiveness of all forms of mass "communication" now make it possible to "create pseudo-public opinion and to undermine democracy from within."[16] Old slogans about *laissez-faire,* which served an important, positive role in their time, are now being used to "justify" practices that are detrimental to creative democracy. The extent to which the entire complex of economic and political institutions can, without controlled direction, create an alienated society that undermines the direct sharing, face-to-face communication, and individual responsibility required for effective democracy was simply not known to the Founding Fathers and not appreciated by nineteenth century liberals. Dewey's plea, made in 1940, for "conscious and resolute effort," is even more relevant at the present time.

But what is the status of the individual for Dewey, and what is the role of individual human freedom in a democratic community? The question not only has important political and moral implications, it also has metaphysical ramifications. Our individuality is grounded in the very nature of what we are. "Preferential action in the sense of selective behavior is a universal trait of all things, atoms and molecules as well as plants, animals and man. Existences, universally as far as we can tell, are cold and indifferent in the presence of some things and react energetically in either a positive or negative way to other things. . . . Selective behavior is evidence of at least rudimentary individuality or uniqueness in things."[17] This generic selective behavior is the basis for understanding what is distinctive about human individuality, viz., choice. "Choice is more than just selectivity in behavior but it is *at least* that."[18]

What else is involved in choice? As we ascend the levels of natural transactions from the inanimate to the animate, and from animals to man, there is an increasing variety and complexity of selective responses. The manifestation of these responses or preferences becomes, with the emergence of man, a function of his entire history. "A man is susceptible, sensitive, to a vast variety of conditions, and undergoes varied and opposed experiences—as lower animals do not."[19] The differences here are differences of degree, for there is continuity throughout all of nature. Not only are human preferences varied and changeable, but conflicting alternative preferences emerge. Out of these conflicting preferences, the formation of a new preference is often demanded in specific practical situations. In understanding the ways in which new preferences are formulated, we come closest to understanding what is distinctive about choice. Observation, foresight, and insight can shape the formation of new desires, preferences, and responses. "In so far as a variable life history and intelligent insight and foresight enter into it, choice signifies a capacity for deliberately changing preferences."[20] Dewey's hypothesis is that these two factors—a variable life history and the possibility of intelligent foresight—are the essential traits of human choice. Human individuality is manifested in choice, and choice itself is dependent on the natural transactions that make up the life history of man and his intelligent deliberations.

> Individuality is at first spontaneous and unshaped; it is potentiality, a capacity of development. Even so, it is a unique manner of acting in and with a world of objects and persons. It is not something complete in itself, like a closet in a house or a secret drawer in a desk, filled with treasures that are waiting to be bestowed on the world. Since individuality is a distinctive way of feeling the im-

> pacts of the world and of showing a preferential bias in response to these impacts, it develops into shape and form only through [transaction] with actual conditions.[21]

Dewey's view of individuality as a potentiality indicates more sharply his dissatisfaction with classic liberalism and points the way to his own positive philosophy of freedom. The trouble with classic liberalism is that it understood man as having a relatively fixed endowment of rights and powers that would be actualized once external restraints were removed. The main problem for classic liberalism is ensuring a minimum of external influence upon the individual by social and political institutions. The real fallacy of classic liberalism "lies in the notion that individuals have such native and original endowment of rights, powers, and wants that all that is required on the side of institutions and laws is to eliminate the obstructions they offer to the free play of the natural equipment of individuals."[22] In its historical context, such a liberalism played an enormous role in challenging and revolutionizing political and social institutions. But as a philosophic position relevant to our new condition, it is defective; classic liberalism fails to realize the powerful influence that all social institutions can exert on subtly shaping the quality and type of human individuality that is expressed. Dewey firmly believed that if complexes of social, economic, and political institutions are not deliberately controlled, they will result in an increase of human alienation and dehumanization. Man can become a creature whose preferences and responses are effectively controlled by forces and powers alien to him. When we appreciate the extent to which the quality of human individuality is affected by the social transactions in which man finds himself, then we are in a position to see what must be done for the creative realization of human individuality. In short, we are on the verge of understanding the role of human freedom.

Freedom is based on the possibility of human choice, but it involves more than this possibility. Freedom requires the effective power to *act* in accord with choice. "There is an intrinsic connection between choice as freedom and the power of action as freedom. A choice which intelligently manifests individuality enlarges the range of action, and this enlargement in turn confers upon our desires greater insight and foresight, and makes choice more intelligent. There is a circle, but an enlarging circle, or, if you please, a widening spiral."[23] This intimate connection between freedom as choice and freedom as the power to act in accord with choice requires the deliberate development of those institutions that will make choice intelligent and action effective. Summing up his view, Dewey writes:

> The possibility of freedom is deeply grounded in our very beings. It is one with our individuality, our being uniquely what we are and not imitators and parasites of others. But like all other possibilities, this possibility has to be actualized; and like all others, it can only be actualized through interaction with objective conditions. The question of political and economic liberty is not an addendum or afterthought, much less a deviation or excrescence, in the problem of personal freedom. For the conditions that form political and economic liberty are required in order to realize the potentiality of freedom each of us carries with him in his very structure.[24]

The entire discussion of individuality, choice and freedom beautifully illustrates the typical pattern of Dewey's thought and reveals the distinctive style of his philosophic investigations. Beginning with a metaphysical analysis of selective behavior which is a characteristic of all existences, Dewey sketches a naturalistic account of the emergence of human choice. This in turn leads him to a consideration of the nature and the effective realization of human freedom—a realization that can be achieved only through the proper transaction with objective conditions as they are embodied in political and economic institutions. Here we see that the highest flight of speculation ends with a distinctively practical turn; there is a continuous movement from theory to practice, from thought to action. Furthermore, the exploration of the nature of valuation, the role of the community—specifically the democratic community—and the analysis of human freedom point us toward the most important medium for social action—education. Philosophy inevitably leads to the theory of education. For Dewey, "if we are willing to conceive education as the process of forming fundamental dispositions, intellectual and emotional, toward nature and fellow men, philosophy may even be defined *as the general theory of education*."[25]

The general theory of education is not a special, peripheral branch of philosophy; it can be identified with the whole of philosophy. For us, this means that when we turn our attention to Dewey's views on education, we are not taking up a special subject, but only making explicit what has been implicit throughout our study of Dewey's philosophy.

In tracing Dewey's intellectual and social development, we have already seen that in Dewey's writings on education he expressed his sharp criticism of the excesses of the "old" and "new" education. He objected to the artificiality and externality of traditional approaches to education that stressed the structure and content of the curriculum, and that looked upon the educational process as one of imposing these studies upon a recalcitrant child. But Dewey was just as critical —and this point cannot be overemphasized, since it is still popularly thought of as Dewey's view—of the excesses of progressive education insofar as it is child-oriented and emphasizes the role of the child in determining what he wants to study. Such a view sentimentalizes and idealizes the child, and fails to appreciate the extent to which a child's experience is immature and crude. Dewey tells us that "doing as one pleases signifies a release from truly *intellectual* initiative and independence," and that when unlimited free expression is allowed, children "gradually tend to become listless and finally bored, while there is an absence of cumulative, progressive development of power and of actual achievement in results."[26] In opposition to this view, Dewey argues for the necessity of deliberate guidance, direction, and order. Education is, or ought to be, a continuous process of reconstruction, in which there is progressive movement away from the child's immature experience to experience that becomes more pregnant with meaning, more systematic and ordered. And what Dewey means by this must be viewed against the background of our entire discussion of the meaning of experience and its transaction with the whole of nature. Such an education can be achieved only through intelligent guidance by the teacher.

The kernel of Dewey's theory of education is reminiscent of the practice of another educator, Socrates. In the early dialogues of Plato, we witness Socrates engaged in conversation with the youths of Athens.

Sensitive to the differences of his interlocutors, and alert to their potentialities and limitations, Socrates skillfully draws upon their natural interests and gradually introduces them to the subtleties of careful analysis. In the *Lysis*, the conversation moves from a discussion of chariots, home life, and friends to an examination of the more abstract and complex subject, the nature of friendship. Socrates is always in control of the dialogue; he uses what is familiar and interesting to Lysis and Menexenus in order to develop their intellectual capacities and lead them to more systematic thinking. What cannot be neglected in Dewey's theory of education, and is usually neglected, is his insistence on clear objectives and skillful guidance in fostering the art of critical thinking, the most difficult of all arts.

It would be insufficient merely to emphasize education as a deliberate reconstruction of experience unless we have a clear idea of what goals, or ends-in-view, are to be achieved. We might sum up the goal under the rubric "intelligence," but this would be an empty term unless we keep in mind the distinctive meaning of intelligence that Dewey has developed throughout his philosophy. We have seen that intelligence is not to be identified with a narrow concept of reason conceived as the ability to make inferences and draw conclusions from explicitly stated premises. Intelligence consists of a set of flexible and growing habits that involve sensitivity; the ability to discern the complexities of situations; imagination that is exercised in seeing new possibilites and hypotheses; willingness to learn from experience; fairness and objectivity in judging and evaluating conflicting values and opinions; and the courage to change one's views when it is demanded by the consequences of our actions. All education is moral education, when we understand "moral" in that broad sense which involves intelligent evaluation. Another way of saying the same thing is that the function of education ought to be to bring about the effective realization of the scientific spirit in all phases of human life. This can be achieved only when the standards required for scientific inquiry become part of the shared life of the community—the democratic community. In our formal educational institutions we must create the type of community which will foster the development of this scientific intelligence. There is no simple or mechanical way of achieving this goal, for the development of intelligence depends upon a subtle transaction with the social environment that the child encounters. The only way in which adults consciously control the kind of education that the immature get is by controlling the environment in which they act. "It is the business of the school environment to eliminate, so far as possible, the unworthy features of the existing environment from influence upon mental habits and attitudes. It establishes a purified medium of action. . . . As a society becomes more enlightened, it realizes that it is responsible *not* to transmit and conserve the whole of its existing achievements, but only such as make for a better future society. The school is its chief agency for the accomplishment of this end."[27] We can clearly see that Dewey did not advocate acquiescence to the *status quo,* or adjustment to existing institutions, as some of his critics have claimed. It is precisely because the school can become the most effective medium for social reform, for making a more intelligent and humane society, that Dewey places such importance on the school. It has become fashionable to criticize American education for being unduly influenced during the last fifty years by Dewey's ideas. But it would be more accurate to say that insofar as our schools have failed to develop the tough-minded habits of intelligence, they have failed to be influenced by what is most basic in Dewey's concept of the function of education in a democratic society.

Chapter 11

THE ARTISTIC, THE ESTHETIC, AND THE RELIGIOUS

In 1934, Dewey published *Art as Experience*. By that time clichés about pragmatism, instrumentalism, and naturalism had become so entrenched, that many followers and critics of Dewey were surprised. After all, wasn't Dewey the philosopher who emphasized means, methods, and instrumentalities rather than ends and esthetic enjoyment? Didn't Dewey ignore the fulfillments and consummations of life in his preoccupation with social and practical problems? One sympathetic critic even asked, "Was Dewey reverting to Hegelianism in his later years? Or had I so widely missed the character of pragmatism that I have seen only half of it, and that perhaps the lesser half?"[1] That is what many interpreters had done—they had missed the essential character of Dewey's concept of pragmatism and of experience. While it is true that in *Art as Experience* Dewey turned to a detailed consideration of the arts, the role of the artistic and the esthetic aspects of experience had been present throughout the development of his theory of experience. Without understanding their function, we are left with a myopic view of Dewey's entire philosophy. We have already suggested the importance of this dimension of Dewey's thought in our discussion of qualitative immediacy and our emphasis on the consummatory phases of all experiences. In *Art as Experience,* Dewey once again took up the issue of experience, restating the fundamentals of his position, showing the rhythm and interpenetration of the instrumental and consummatory phases of experience.

We can approach Dewey's theory of art and esthetic experience by participating in his dialectic with Greek philosophy. While the Greek philosophers had a sensitive appreciation of the esthetic dimension of life, Dewey argues that they were guilty of confusing esthetic and rational categories. In our earlier discussion of the Greek view of experience, we noted the presence of the distinction between the practical and the theoretical. The "practical," especially in Aristotle's scheme, designates the arts of doing and making, while the "theoretical" is concerned with knowing and ultimately knowing in its highest form—contemplation. "Art was born of need, lack, deprivation, incompleteness, while science—theory—manifested fullness and totality of Being. Thus the depreciatory view of experience was identical with a conception that placed practical activity below theoretical activity, finding the former dependent, impelled from the outside, marked by deficiency of real being, while the latter was independent and free because complete and self-sufficing: that is perfect."[2] The highest type of knowledge is the contemplation of perfect forms or universals. The process of knowing is consummated by a pure contemplation of being or reality. "Greek philosophy as well as Greek art is a memorial of the joy in what is finished, when it is found amid a world of unrest, struggle, and uncertainty in what, since it is ended, does not commit us to the uncertain hazards of what is still going on."[3] Dewey's criticism is that the Greeks confused the immediate enjoyment of meanings and values which is characteristic of the esthetic dimension of experience with knowing or cognitive experience. The Greeks hypostasized objects of immediate enjoyment into a transcendent reality. "Such was the conversion of Greek esthetic contemplation effected by Greek reflection."[4] In the background of their view of knowing as contemplation is a metaphor of the spectator view of knowledge. Using this has dominated a good deal of philosophy. Using this metaphor, one conceives of the ultimate act of knowing as the contemplation or "seeing" in which the object of knowledge is illuminated. This is the metaphor or model for knowing that Dewey has criticized throughout his writings, replacing it with a view of knowing as it functions in ongoing self-corrective inquiry. Though Dewey thinks that there were good reasons for such a view of the cosmos in Greek civilization, we now require a transformation of this outlook; it is a transformation in the sense that we must now develop a *new* interpretation for the insights that were articulated in the Greek view of things.

The doctrine that ends, being the ultimate forms of reality, are the proper objects of true science, "met its doom in the scientific revolution of the Seventeenth Century. . . . Essences and forms were attacked as occult; 'final causes' were either wholly denied or relegated to a divine realm too high for human knowledge. The doctrine of natural ends was displaced by a doctrine of designs, ends-in-view, conscious aims constructed and entertained in individual minds independent of nature."[5] When the influence of modern physics penetrated, the classic theory of forms and ends became remote, faded, and discarded. But, as we have seen in the discussion of immediate quality, the new "scientific philosophy" contained its own paradoxes. The status of immediate endings became a philosophic perplexity. There seemed to be no place for them in an objective, public, scientific world; the very qualities which the Greeks deemed the highest expression of reality were now condemned to the private, the subjective, the merely mental. Dewey asks, "Is this reversal of classic theories of existence inevitable? Must belief in ends involved in nature itself be surrendered, or be asserted only by means of a roundabout examination of the nature of knowledge which, starting from conscious intent to know, finally infers that the universe is a vast, non-natural fulfillment of a conscious intent? Or is there an ingredient of truth in ancient metaphysics which may be extracted and reaffirmed?"[6] Dewey most certainly does believe that there is an element of truth in Greek metaphysics, but if we are to extract it then we must appreciate how the development of experimental science has transformed our intellectual scene. The most important lesson that is to be learned from this development is that the Greek distinction between theory and practice is no longer warranted. Experimental science has taught us that scientific knowing is a form of activity, a practice—an art. Dewey's theory of inquiry has centered about this fundamental change and is an attempt to articulate the ways in which knowing is an art. In short, the distinction between, on one hand, theory or knowing as contemplation and, on the other, practice or art as limited to lesser forms of doing and making, can no longer be maintained. When the implications of the new way of understanding inquiry and its role in human life are fully developed, Dewey claims:

> It would then be seen that science is an art, that art is practice, and that the only distinction worth drawing is not between practice and theory, but between those modes of practice that are not intelligent, not inherently and immediately enjoyable, and those which are full of enjoyed meanings. When this perception dawns, it will be a commonplace that art—the mode of activity that is charged with meanings capable of immediately enjoyed possession—is the complete culmination of nature, and that "science" is properly a handmaiden that conducts natural events to this happy issue. Thus would disappear the separations that trouble present thinking; division of everything into nature *and* experience, of experience into practice *and* theory, art *and* science, of art into useful *and* fine, menial *and* free.[7]

If the notion of practice or art must be enlarged in order to include not only what the Greeks recognized as art but also the art of knowing in all its varieties, then what place, if any, is there for the contemplative enjoyment of ends which they took to be the highest form of knowing? The above passage suggests the answer. For the Greeks were right in appreciating the importance of consummations, of the direct esthetic enjoyment of immediate qualities. But these qualities are not expressions of a transcendent reality, nor is this esthetic enjoyment a form of *knowing*. Consummations, and the direct enjoyment of esthetic quality, must be understood in the rhythm of experience. There can be a rhythm in experience, a movement from the conflicts and problems that emerge in the ongoing process of experience toward fulfillments and consummations of these experiences. These are the endings or consummations *within* experience. As such they are natural endings, not endings that are already fixed in a determinate hierarchy, but endings realized through the directed transformation of experience. Not only can all inquiry and all life be understood as art—a controlled activity—but esthetic quality is not limited to a special type of experience: it can pervade all experiences. There is a consummatory phase of scientific inquiry just as there is one in deliberative valuation. Every integral experience, everything which is distinctively *an* experience, moves toward a close, an ending, a fulfillment. Consequently, "the enemies of the esthetic are neither the practical nor the intellectual. They are the humdrum; slackness of loose ends; submission to convention in practice and intellectual procedure. Rigid abstinence, coerced submission, tightness on one side and dissipation, incoherence and aimless indulgence on the other, are deviations in opposite directions from the unity of an experience."[8]

From this point of view, the "artistic" as production and the "esthetic" as fulfillment and consummation are concepts applicable to all experiences; they are not limited to a special type of experience. Furthermore, there is the prescription in Dewey's philosophy that *all* experience ought to be made more artistic and esthetic. The experiences that we think of as distinctively esthetic differ in degree from other experiences, not in kind. "There are situations in which self-enclosed, discrete, individualized characters dominate. They constitute the subject-matter of esthetic experience; and every experience is esthetic in so far as it is final, or arouses no search for some other experience. When this complete quality is conspicuous the experience is denominated esthetic."[9]

The significance of Dewey's position concerning the

mutual dependence of the artistic and the esthetic in all experience can be further clarified by considering his claim of the continuum of means and ends. The specific view that Dewey criticizes is one that makes a sharp distinction between means and ends and thinks of means as completely independent of ends. "Means" and "ends" do not refer to different grades of reality or being. They refer to the *same* reality, as it is conceived from different perspectives. A simple illustration brings out Dewey's point. When a person is building a house, the end-in-view is not some remote or final goal which is hit upon after performing a series of disconnected acts. "The end-in-view is a plan which is *contemporaneously* operative in selecting and arranging materials. The latter, brick, stone, wood, and mortar, are means only as the end-in-view is actually incarnate in them, in forming them. Literally, they *are* the end in its present stage of realization. The end-in-view is present at each stage of the process; it is present as the *meaning* of the materials used and acts done; without its informing presence, the latter are in no sense 'means'; they are merely extrinsic causal conditions."[10] And while the completion of the house is the end or fulfillment of the acts involved in building it, and consequently is a consummation relative to the specific situation, it can function as a means in some further experience. Means, then, are not things that are only external and accidental antecedents of the happening of something else, just as ends are not independent of what has come before. "A genuine instrumentality *for* is always an organ *of* an end."[11] In answer to the criticism that the continuum of means and ends leads to a hopeless *regressus ad infinitum* because there is no end that is not also a means, Dewey tells us that we must always look to the specific context in which means and ends are distinguished.[12] Apart from situations in which there is a tension between a person and his environing conditions, there would be no occasion for forming ends-in-view and the means for realizing the consequences that are chosen as ends. In a given situation there are finalities and consummations; but a consummation is the resolution and fulfillment of a *specific* tensional situation. There is a great difference between a quality of finality and a final quality.

But what is the point of this analysis of means and ends, and how is it related to the "artistic" and the "esthetic"? The discussion of means and ends is not just a technical philosophic issue: some of our profoundest social and practical problems reflect an artificial divorce between means and ends. For example, we speak of labor or work as a means to earning a livelihood, and will frequently justify the boring, stultifying aspects of work as being a necessary "means" for the "end" of earning a living. When we divorce the instrumental from the consummatory, ends frequently become indulgent dissipations, passive amusements and distractions. "The notion that means are menial, instrumentalities servile, is more than a degradation of means to the rank of coercive and external necessities. It renders all things upon which the name of end is bestowed accompaniments of privilege, while the name of utility becomes an apologetic justification for things that are not portions of a good and reasonable life."[13] Dewey was no sentimentalist who thought that it was possible for man to find joy in everything that he does. But he did believe that the divorce between means and ends that is so prevalent in our society and that results in the alienation of man could be overcome so that man could find *greater* joy, satisfaction, and esthetic significance in what he does. Life and experience can become more artistic and esthetic when there is a genuine interpenetration of means and ends —when we do not treat means as mere or as external necessities, but as modes of activity inherently and immediately enjoyable, which are full of enjoyed meanings and values—and when ends are not simply final points to be reached in a far-off future, but are genuine consummations and fulfillments in which means are integrated.

Any activity that is simultaneously productive and esthetic, instrumental, and consummatory is art. Art, therefore, is at once a natural event and the completion of nature. "Thought, intelligence, science is the intentional direction of natural events to meanings capable of immediate possession and enjoyment; this direction—which is operative art—is itself a natural event in which nature otherwise partial and incomplete comes fully to itself; so that objects of conscious experience, when reflectively chosen, form the 'end' of nature."[14]

Thus far we have been treating the "artistic" and the "esthetic" from a generic perspective; from a perspective in which these concepts are applicable to all experience, whether it be dominantly intellectual or practical. Dewey, of course, recognizes that there is a more common and specific meaning of art, in which works of art are the end-product. This mode of activity is continuous with the "artistic" and the "esthetic" as they are manifested in all experience. But to say that it is continuous is not to deny that it has a unique function. We cannot here present a detailed discussion of Dewey's analysis of the various arts, but we can highlight some of the main points of his analysis.

Art as a distinctive activity culminates in a work of art. A work of art is not to be identified with the art product (a statue, painting, etc.). The latter is physical and potential, while the former is active and experienced. The art product is a work of art only insofar as it is viewed as the culmination of the transactions of the artist or creator and only insofar as it enters into active transaction with the observer-participant (even if this is the artist himself). A work of art is re-created every time it is esthetically experienced. Consequently, a work of art is complete only insofar as it enters into the experience of those who actively share and participate in it. "Through art, meanings of objects that are otherwise dumb, inchoate, restricted, and resisted are clarified and concentrated, and not by thought working laboriously upon them, nor by escape into a world of mere sense, but by the creation of a new experience."[15] The artist, of course, can create such a new experience only through a concrete medium. What he can say in the language of art is limited by the medium in which he works. Artistic genius is revealed in the ability to fund sensuous qualities with meaning and value. The material out of which a work of art is created includes the meanings, values, and emotions extracted from past experience. As such this material "belongs to the common world rather than to the self, and yet there is self-expression in art because the self assimilates that material in a distinctive way to reissue it into the public world in a form that builds a new object."[16] The meanings and values imbued in a work of art are expressed, or shown, rather than stated or said. This distinction between expressing and stating meaning is extremely important. While art has meaning, we only confuse the significance of this meaning if we apply criteria that are applicable to scientific inquiry to art. Science states meanings, while art expresses them. This is not to say that the purpose of art or the artist is to communicate; communication is a *consequence* of a work of art. "In the end, works of art are the only media of complete and unhindered communication between man and man that can occur in a world full of gulfs and walls that limit community of experience."[17] Irwin Edman has summed up Dewey's philosophy of art when he writes:

> The arts are modes of experiencing, in which through the imaginative use of a medium, the organization of color, light, line, sound, all the resources of the arts, the liveness of live creature is enlivened, and his liveness given a vital order through form. The arts are modes of energy which function as ways of communication. But the communication of art is something far different than conveying practical information or stating general and abstract ideas. Art communicates by celebrating the qualities of human experience. Its celebration is through the delight, at once perspicuous and vivid, of patterned energies, ordered experience. Art communicates because it renders available in clear and heightened unities the qualities of experience that are seen with absorption and heard as direct and as delightful. The special way in which art communicates is through the operation of imagination as Dewey conceives it. The arts present in each genuine (not merely academic and repetitive) instance, a new experience.[18]

Art as the embodiment of creative imagination can play an enormous role in the development of civilization. Dewey quotes with approval Shelley's statement, "The imagination is the great instrument of moral good. . . ."[19] Art has a moral function in civilization, but not by being moralistic or didactic. The moral function of art is exercised by the imaginative projection and presentation of ideals. "The moral prophets of humanity have always been the poets even though they spoke in free verse or by parable."[20] Paradoxically, Dewey claims that art is more moral than moralities. The latter frequently tend to become consecrations of the *status quo* and reinforcements of the established order. "Art has been the means of keeping alive the sense of purposes that outrun evidence and of meanings that transcend indurated habit."[21]

This discussion of art at once echoes back to our original exploration of Dewey's concept of philosophy and points the way to his discussion of the religious attitude and quality. Philosophy is not only like the arts, it is an art. We have pointed out that philosophy is primarily concerned with meaning rather than truth, though truth is of crucial importance for philosophy. "In philosophy we are dealing with something comparable to the meaning of Athenian civilization or of a drama." The type of meaning that is the concern of philosophy is meaning as it is expressed or exhibited in a work of art. We also noted the importance of imagination in philosophy. For the philosopher must take up the disordered fragments, uncompleted meanings and values that he inherits, and imaginatively reconstruct them into a whole that is more coherent and unified. As such the methods of philosophy should be scientific, and the culmination of philosophy as an activity is a work of art—a work of art that has the power to enrich and enliven all aspects of human experience. In "Philosophy and Civilization," Dewey decries the contemporary "worship" of science. His plea is for the reconstruction of philosophy as an art. "As far as any plea is implicit in what has been said, it is, then, a plea for the casting off of that intellectual timidity which hampers the wings of imagination, a plea for speculative audacity, for more faith in ideas, sloughing off a cowardly reliance upon those partial ideas to which we are wont to give the name facts. I have given to philosophy a more humble function than that which is often assigned it. But modesty as to its final place is not incompatible with boldness in the maintenance of that function, humble as it may be. A combination of such modesty and courage affords the only way I know of in which the philosopher can look his fellowman in the face with frankness and with humanity."[22]

The exploration of the artistic and esthetic aspects of experience brings us to the point where we can examine the religious dimension of experience. We can thereby round out our study of Dewey's comprehensive philosophy. It should be clear by now that there is a reason for the adjectival force of the terms "artistic," "esthetic," and "religious." The main thrust of Dewey's theory of experience has been that experience is qualified in multifarious ways. The above adjectives designate distinctive ways in which *any* experience can be qualified. This is especially important in Dewey's discussion of the religious because he wants to distinguish carefully the religious attitude or quality from its specific embodiment in religions. At the same time Dewey is critical of the notion of a special type of religious experience that can be neatly separated from other types of experience. But before turning directly to what Dewey does mean by the religious attitude, it is desirable to place his inquiry in the perspective of his entire philosophic endeavor.

In surveying the enormous body of Dewey's writings, which cover a period of three generations, one is struck by the paucity of explicit treatment of religious issues. Dewey tells us quite honestly, in his autobiographical sketch, "I was brought up in a conventionally evangelical atmosphere of the more 'liberal' sort; and the struggles that later arose between acceptance of that faith and the discarding of traditional and institutional creeds came from personal experiences and not from the effects of philosophical teaching. It was not, in other words, in this respect that philosophy either appealed to me or influenced me."[23] It might even be said that Dewey's early interest in philosophy, especially Hegel, provided an intellectual alternative and liberation from the personal crisis of faith that he suffered. "While the conflict of traditional religious beliefs with opinions that I could myself honestly entertain was the source of a trying personal crisis, it did not at any time constitute a leading philosophical problem. This might look as if the two things were kept apart; in reality it was due to a feeling that any genuinely sound religious experience could and should adapt itself to whatever beliefs one found oneself intellectually entitled to hold—a half unconscious sense at first, but one which ensuing years have deepened into a fundamental conviction."[24] Consequently, Dewey admits, "I have never been able to attach much importance to religion as a philosophic problem."[25]

Nevertheless Dewey did turn his attention to the discussion of religion in the Terry Lectures delivered at Yale in 1934 and published in *A Common Faith.* Did Dewey change his mind about the importance of religion as a philosophic problem? Was he now attempting to show that he, too, had a "philosophy of religion"? *A Common Faith* has been read in this way and is usually subjected to severe criticism. I want to suggest, however, that it is a mistake to read *A Common Faith* as Dewey's *new* philosophy of religion. It is rather an expression of what might be called Dewey's "natural piety." Interpreted in this manner, Dewey is making explicit what is implicit in his entire philosophy. In this sense, Dewey's treatment of the religious attitude and quality is the culmination of his entire philosophy. We discover here how the pieces "add up," and how Dewey viewed man in relation to the universe that he encounters.

Dewey maintains that there is no such thing as religion in the singular; there are only a multitude of religions. Furthermore, he thinks that the attempt to find a significant, central meaning in these religions—something essential that all religions share—is doomed to failure. "A religion . . . always signifies a special body of beliefs and practices having some kind of institutional organization, loose or tight."[26] It is not even necessary for religions to be concerned with a supernatural or transcendent being, although this has been characteristic of the major religions in the Western tradition. Dewey is skeptical of the knowledge claims made in the name of various religions. There is no higher authority than the authority of inquiry itself. "The new methods of inquiry and reflection have become for the educated man today the final arbiter of all questions of fact, existence, and intellectual assent. Nothing less than a revolution in the 'seat of intellectual authority' has taken place. . . . The mind of man is being habituated to a new method and ideal. There is but one sure road of access to truth—the road of patient, cooperative inquiry operating by means of observation, experiment, record, and controlled reflection."[27] Religion, then, is not a "higher" or a separate, other seat of intellectual authority; faith is not a "higher" form of knowledge. For some, this denial of religion as a source of authority will be tantamount to atheism. If this is what one means by atheism, then Dewey is an atheist. But he did not think so. He thought that there is a religious attitude or quality of experience that could and indeed should be carefully distinguished from religions in their institutional forms. But, having said this, we must be careful to distinguish Dewey's position from those who have taken religious experience to be the quintessence of religion.

When philosophers and theologians have spoken of religious experience, they have frequently fused (Dewey claims they have *con*fused) two things that must be carefully distinguished. There is no doubt that there are extremely intense and momentous experiences, which have changed men's lives. We may feel a sense of harmony with the universe, or a profound joy at the wonder and mystery of the universe, or a resolution of our most basic anxieties and personal conflicts in a new experience. One cannot doubt the existence of such experiences, but the way in which such experiences are to be interpreted is quite a different matter. Too frequently the interpretation that is immediately given to the significance of these momentous experiences is one conditioned by the values and framework implicit in a given cultural setting. But to claim that the experience is proof, justification, or evidence for some specific religious doctrine is to make an unwarranted leap from the experience to a specific interpretation of it. "The particular interpretation given to this complex of conditions is not inherent in the experience itself. It is derived from the culture with which a particular person has been imbued."[28]

But what are the distinctive features of the religious

attitude that distinguish it from its embodiment in specific historic religions and from so-called religious experiences? The religious attitude is one that involves a fundamental change in our conscious relation to the entire universe. It is a change that pertains to our entire being or self; it is an attitude that involves a note of submission and is at the same time voluntary. It is an attitude in which there is a thoroughgoing harmonizing of the *whole* "self with the Universe (as a name for the totality of conditions with which the self is connected)."[29] A religious attitude requires faith, but "faith" takes on a new meaning in this context: "I should describe this faith as the unification of the self through allegiance to inclusive ideal ends, which imagination presents to us and to which the human will responds as worthy of controlling our desires and choices."[30] It is important to emphasize that ends or ideals are ultimately chosen by man; man chooses ideals he considers worthy of controlling the guidance of his life. As such, ends or ideals are not fixed parts of a reality that is completely independent of us. Ideals that are imaginatively conceived are real in the sense that they have an undeniable power in action. "We are in the presence neither of ideals completely embodied in existence nor yet of ideals that are mere rootless ideals, fantasies, utopias. For there are forces in nature and society that generate and support the ideals. They are further unified by the action that gives them coherence and validity."[31] It is this active relation between the ideal and the actual that Dewey calls God. It might be thought that Dewey's use of "God" is a complete departure from the way in which God has been conceived of as the Supreme Being or the Ground of all Being. Dewey is rejecting this tradition. But his concept of God as the unity of all ideal ends that stand in active relation to us is in the spirit (though not the letter) of Kant's concept of God. Kant carefully distinguished the ontological issue of God's existence—something which we can never *know*—from the practical significance of God as a regulative ideal for all human experience and action. For Dewey, "God" is the name of a regulative ideal.

We can now see why Dewey's concept of the "religious" might well be called an expression of natural piety and is a culmination of his entire philosophy. Man is that creature who is at once part of the totality of nature and continuous with natural transactions, but who can also intervene in the course of nature, direct it, imagine and achieve new ends. Man is limited by and dependent on nature, and the religious attitude requires a sense of this dependence. "The essentially unreligious attitude is that which attributes human achievement and purpose to man in isolation from the world of physical nature and his fellows."[32] But this awareness of our finitude need not result in despair, fatalism, or the stoical acceptance of the existing mixture of evil and good. We are creatures capable of intelligence, of imaginatively conceiving new directions and ideals for reconstructing existing conditions. We are emotional and passionate creatures capable of supreme loyalty to those flexible goals that we deem worthy of guiding our lives.

This is what Dewey has been telling us throughout his philosophic investigations, and this is what he sums up in his discussion of the religious attitude. "Natural piety is not of necessity either a fatalistic acquiescence in natural happenings or a romantic idealization of the world. It may rest upon a just sense of nature as the whole of which we are parts, while it also recognizes that we are parts that are marked by intelligence and purpose, having the capacity to strive by their aid to bring conditions into greater consonance with what is humanly desirable."[33]

Such a natural piety finds its fullest expression in the life of the community, for it is through the community that values are shared and ideals that we envision can become effective. Dewey's faith in the possibilities and future of the community are summed up in the concluding passage of *A Common Faith*:

> We who now live are parts of a humanity that extends into the remote past, a humanity that has interacted with nature. The things in civilization we most prize are not of ourselves. They exist by grace of the doings and sufferings of the continuous human community in which we are a link. Ours is the responsibility of conserving, transmitting, rectifying, and expanding the heritage of values we have received that those who come after us may receive it more solid and secure, more widely accessible and more generously shared than we have received it. Here are all the elements for a religious faith that shall not be confined to sect, class, or race. Such a faith has always been implicitly the common faith of mankind. It remains to make it explicit and militant.[34]

Chapter 12

RETROSPECTIVE AND PROSPECTIVE

It is difficult to believe that Dewey died just less than fifteen years ago. We associate his ideas with the period from the turn of the century until the beginning of the New Deal, and it was then that he enjoyed the greatest popularity and had the greatest influence. I have argued that Dewey's most important and enduring work was done after 1925, but by that time many philosophers had ceased reading him seriously, or had interpreted his work through the distorted image of popular clichés about "pragmatism" and "progressive education." Since the Second World War, there has been very little serious critical discussion of his philosophy. Dewey has become a favorite whipping boy. If we are to gain some critical distance for the purpose of evaluating Dewey's contribution, it becomes necessary to examine what has happened to philosophy in America. We can chart its course by exploring the significance of four different trends in recent philosophy: logical empiricism and the philosophy of science; the variety of linguistic analysis practiced in England; the existentialist and phenomenological movements; and the persistence of a small but articulate group of philosophers working in a bold, metaphysical tradition.

It is during the thirties that we can detect the first signs of a significant alternative to Dewey's broad, humane naturalism. In part, this was due to an accident of fate, for it was a time of the influx of refugee philosophers who came to America to escape the rise of Nazi Germany. Of this group, those whose impact was felt most strongly were the logical positivists or, as they are sometimes called, the logical empiricists. Most of them had been associated with the famed Vienna Circle that had attempted to put philosophy, once and for all, on a scientific basis. Logical empiricism found a congenial home in America, and to a large extent this was because of Dewey's influence. A persistent theme in Dewey's philosophy had been the importance of science and scientific method for all aspects of philosophy. Dewey had called for a specific investigation of the nature of science and had expressed his skepticism of speculative metaphysics. To many it seemed that positivism, with its close alliance with the philosophy of science and its insistence on the verifiability principle of meaning, was not only compatible with the pragmatic tradition but was a further development of this same tradition. After all, many of the positivists had been scientists and had the technical equipment and knowledge to analyze the structure of science, especially the physical sciences, that Dewey himself had lacked. It is still a popular myth, even among philosophers, that positivism was a tough-minded variety of the more tender-minded and fuzzy pragmatism. The uneasy alliance of pragmatism and positivism can be seen in the publications of the *International Encyclopedia of Unified Science*, of which Otto Neurath was editor-in-chief and Rudolf Carnap was an associate editor. Both

Neurath and Carnap had been members of the Vienna Circle. The "American side" was represented by Charles Morris, also an associate editor, who had been a student of G. H. Mead. Morris, in his own monograph on *Foundations of the Theory of Signs,* set forth the common platform of positivism and pragmatism. Dewey himself was invited to join forces and wrote his *Theory of Valuation* for the *Encyclopedia.* A careful reading of this monograph, especially Dewey's criticism of the positivists' doctrine of emotivism—the doctrine that normative ethical judgments are not really judgments at all, but rather the expression of emotive preferences and attitudes—might have shown that all was not well in this joining of pragmatism and positivism.

What was then not clearly seen, and is today still barely recognized, is the deep antagonism between logical positivism and pragmatism. Positivism was not just a philosophic position concerned with the application of symbolic logic to philosophic problems and with an analysis of the structure of science. Positivism claimed "finally" to put an end to nonsense by proposing a rigid criterion for meaningful discourse. Though radical in its stance, it harbored many epistemological orthodoxies. The theory of sense data; the rigid distinction between the analytic and the synthetic, observation and theory, the cognitive and the noncognitive; the nominalistic and atomistic proclivities of its proponents, the ideal of a complete reduction of all empirical concepts to the basic atomistic elements of experience, lay at the foundation of positivism. Many of these dogmas were refined versions of ideas implicit in the empiricist tradition. They are the very dogmas that Dewey had severely attacked. At the heart of logical positivism was the concept of experience that Dewey had set out to correct. His own contextualistic theory of experience as a transaction of organism-environment pervaded by a unifying quality was intended to be an alternative to the emasculated theory of experience implicit in both traditional empiricism and the new logical empiricism. It is no accident that except for the initial contribution of "emotivism," which has now been completely abandoned or modified beyond recognition, logical positivism has not made any significant contribution to our understanding of the value dimension of human experience. Positivism lacked a rich enough theory of experience to make such a contribution. In sum, despite a superficial agreement between pragmatism and positivism, positivism contained an outdated and outmoded epistemology—an epistemology that Dewey had both criticized and sought to replace with a more adequate theory of experience and inquiry.

The early epistemological dogmas of positivism, which seemed so striking and persuasive, have now been almost totally rejected. The real legacy of this movement is to be found in the philosophy of science. Twenty-five years ago there was virtually no philosophy of science that was independent of the rest of philosophy. Today, the philosophy of science has become a special field; there is hardly a first-rate university in America that doesn't have its "specialist" in the philosophy of science, and throughout the country special programs and institutes dedicated exclusively to the philosophy of science have sprung up.

The internal development of the philosophy of science has been a curious one. In its most recent developments, the very dogmas which had been the cornerstone of the positivist conception of science have been severely criticized. Positivism had been a variety of that type of philosophy that emphasizes rigid distinctions, but every one of these "dualisms" has now been rejected or modified, whether it be the distinction between observation and theory, analytic and synthetic, or sense and thought. A new spirit has emerged, one that emphasizes the context of scientific inquiry rather than the results and the formal structure of the logic of proof and confirmation. Throughout all this there has been an appreciation for the open-textured dimension of inquiry, and an emphasis on flexibility, on functional rather than rigid distinctions. A pragmatic spirit, the spirit of Dewey, pervades the new philosophy of science. It would be misleading to claim that this is a direct result of Dewey's influence, though some of the philosophers pioneering this effort have recognized their affinity to the pragmatic tradition and to Dewey. It would be more accurate to say that philosophers of science have come to see in a detailed and more precise way what Dewey too often left in a rather general and suggestive manner.

This spirit of Dewey's thought in the recent philosophy of science indicates some of the significant strengths and weaknesses of Dewey's philosophy. Dewey was a philosopher of great insight, and his general view of the nature of scientific inquiry is now being vindicated by piecemeal and specialized investigation. Dewey lacked the technical skill and patience to develop and establish his insights in systematic detail. Dewey was a philosopher who painted with a broad stroke; he was a man of vision and fertile imagination. Without these qualities a philosophy can become scholastic, academic, and pointless. But imagination and insight must be explicated and modified in detailed analyses, and this is what Dewey failed to do for us. Insofar as philosophy requires the funding of fertile imagination with systematic elaboration, his philosophy fails.

Dewey's strength is in his constant attempt to relate science and scientific inquiry to the larger human scene, to understand its import and consequences for man in his encounters with nature. Unfortunately, the new philosophy of science has frequently neglected the broader context of science (though this is not universally true). There is a danger that this discipline can become "scholastic"—in the derogatory sense of the term. Dewey's philosophic vision stands as a warning and a challenge to explore and appreciate the general import of scientific inquiry and to make the scientific spirit relevant to other dimensions of human experience and philosophic inquiry.

The second main influence on the course of American philosophy since Dewey has been the movement of linguistic analysis as practiced mainly in England. Unlike positivism, which began with an explicit and well-defined program, this is a movement in which the commonness is to be found in a temper, a mood, a mode of approach rather than a set of common philosophic theses. Undoubtedly the key figure has been Wittgenstein. Sometimes this movement is called "ordinary-language philosophy," but although the discussion of the "logic" of ordinary language has been in the foreground, I think that when we are able to look at this movement in perspective, the emphasis on ordinary language will be seen as having secondary importance only. Wittgenstein is a difficult philosopher to classify: his whole style of philosophy is antithetical to such treatment. He was a man obsessed with what it is that makes us philosophize and what it is that leads us to "false" solutions and pictures. His *Philosophical Investigations* might have been subtitled *A Critique of*

Philosophy, and in this respect he is reminiscent of Kant, who was also concerned with understanding the limits of what we can think and the reason why we attempt to transcend these limits. Aside from this general orientation, there are many aspects of the mood and emphasis of Wittgenstein and linguistic analysis that have close affinities with Dewey. Wittgenstein, in his later writings, was reacting against the excesses of positivism and logical atomism that had dominated philosophy during the early part of the twentieth century. Instead of looking and seeing what is actually the case, philosophers had attempted to impose an ideal of what our language and thought must be like. As a result, our language and thought were not clarified—rather, they were distorted by "ideal" demands of what they should be like. Dewey too had initially rebelled against the excesses of formalism, static categories, and the demands of atomism and reductionism. In place of this artificial characterization of experience, the new movement of linguistic analysis has attempted to show how our language and thereby our thought is open-textured and inescapably (though not hopelessly) vague. Linguistic context is emphasized, but language includes not just words and sentences but the entire complex of activities, assumptions, and beliefs that make up the context.

Furthermore, in Wittgenstein and linguistic analysis there is a definite anti-Cartesian and anti-subjectivist bias. Here too there are strong family resemblances with the pragmatic movement and Dewey. Wittgenstein, more effectively than Dewey, showed how misleading it can be to try to "explain" such concepts as meaning, understanding, thinking, and even our reference to such "private experiences" as pain by appealing to mental events, processes, or subjective awareness. Like Dewey, Wittgenstein was not advocating an extreme behaviorism that attempts a reduction of all "mental talk" to talk about publicly observable objects and events. We find a new way of viewing language and thought, which undercuts a simple dichotomy of the mental and the physical, a new way that emphasizes language games, contexts, forms of life, and conjoint activities.

The differences between Wittgenstein and Dewey are as striking as the similarities. Perhaps the main differences stem from their different concepts of philosophy. Philosophy as an activity, according to Wittgenstein, describes and does not explain. Philosophy as a therapeutic activity does not solve problems, it helps to dissolve them. We have succeeded when we can escape philosophizing, and when we realize how false pictures and expectations mislead us. There have not been many philosophers who have adopted Wittgenstein's extreme concept of philosophy, but there have been many who have made dogmatic slogans of what are tentative stages in Wittgenstein's investigations. Although Wittgenstein did not attempt to apply his techniques to our discourse about ethics, esthetics, and religion, there have been many who think that this is where his techniques are most fruitful. Since the Second World War there has been a new passion to describe the complex structure of our discourse about values without imposing alien ideals and norms.

It is in this area of investigation that we detect some of the sharpest differences between the spirit of this movement and the spirit of Dewey's philosophy. Dewey was a confessed moralist, although he was not moralistic. He did not dogmatically sermonize, but everything he did and wrote is pervaded with a sense that the philosopher's primary task is to reconstruct and direct the course of human experience and culture. Philosophy is not simply a mode of description; it is criticism, and this criticism is to function in the widest, most humane context. Dewey would have abhorred the new dogma that has emerged from linguistic analysis, that the ethical philosopher's task is essentially completed when he has sympathetically and accurately described the complex ways in which we argue and reason about moral issues. He would, of course, be sympathetic with the need to do this as a propaedeutic to the critical function of philosophy, but certainly not as an end in itself. Here, too, the strengths and weaknesses of Dewey come to the foreground. For as a result of recent investigations in ethics, we have come to a much clearer understanding of the complexity of moral discourse. Dewey spoke about this complexity, but did very little to illuminate it in detail and left us with a few general indications. But I can see no warrant for the belief that the philosopher's task is done when he has described moral discourse, and that the specific criticism and prescription are the function of somebody else. Such an artificial division of labor can have dangerous consequences, for it can lead to the abdication of the philosopher's role—a role that has its roots in Plato—as the rational critic. In this area, too, Dewey stands as a challenge to make philosophy relevant to the "problems of men."

The third influence that has affected the philosophic scene in America in a post-Deweyean period has been that of existentialism and, more recently, phenomenology. Originally the influence of this movement was most directly felt in our theological seminaries; it is only during the past few years that this movement has been seriously studied in our academic philosophy departments. The growing influence of this movement coincided with the moral and social disruption accompanying the rise of Nazism. Paul Tillich and Reinhold Niebuhr have been the most influential advocates of religious existentialism in America. Niebuhr's own development is a good barometer of the change in social climate that took place in America during the First and Second World Wars that resulted in disaffection for Dewey's ideas and a caricature of his philosophy. The young Niebuhr was with Dewey in spirit and shared Dewey's faith in democracy and his commitment to social action as the means for eliminating existing evils. But Niebuhr, who was at once a leader and a representative of an entire generation of religious thinkers in America, came to feel the inadequacies of what he took to be Dewey's liberal faith. Dewey, it was proclaimed, had a shallow sense of human nature and lacked a "tragic sense" of the human condition. Dewey failed to realize that the ultimate source of personal frustration and unhappiness stems from man's religious alienation in the modern world and cannot be resolved through social action only, but requires religious faith. "Commitment," "anxiety," "existential absurdity," "death," and "decision" became the issues and problems prominent from this existential perspective. These are really the "problems of men," and Dewey's philosophy seemed to have little to say about them.

I do not think that it can be denied that Dewey did have an optimistic outlook, and that he did believe that the day would come when intelligence would pervade the democratic community through the medium of education. I also think that the weakest part of Dewey's entire philosophy is his analysis of the self—the focal point of the existentialist and phenomenological movement. Dewey even admitted (though it is scientific psychology that he has in mind) that "I have failed to develop in a systematic way my underlying psychological principles."[1] But we must not confuse the temper of the man with the resources of his philosophic point of view. Dewey was certainly aware of the limitedness and finitude of man. There are no ultimate values that are given to man, and there is no ultimate purpose to the universe. Value comes into existence only when man appears on the scene, and it is up to him to make his life meaningful and valuable. Failure and frustration are inevitable parts of human life. To wish them away is to engage in fantasy. The crucial issue is what is to be our reaction to the evils that do exist and the frustrations that are so much a part of our lives. Let us grant all that the existentialists have told us about the irreducible absurdity of the world in which we live. Still, we cannot escape making decisions and choices. The question then becomes, how is this to be done? Dewey's entire philosophy is an argument that the method of intelligence is our best resource and guide for living. In the end, the labels of "optimism" and "pessimism" are irrelevant to assessing Dewey's outlook. The greater our awareness of the alienation that affects so much of man's life, the greater the challenge to make intelligence effective. Dewey's imperative certainly lacks the glamour of more extremist philosophies, but his sane, piecemeal approach to reconstruction of human experience is undoubtedly a more realistic and ultimately more effective guide for meeting our problems and making human existence more livable.

We have stressed the moral and social dimension of the existentialist and phenomenological tradition, for, unlike the varieties of academic philosophy that have been most influential in America after Dewey, this movement has shared Dewey's concern with moral and social action. There is also a good deal in common between Dewey and phenomenology, especially in its recent developments. For this movement, too, has rebelled against the mind-body dualism implicit in the Cartesian tradition of modern philosophy. As the works of the phenomenologists are being translated into English, it is becoming increasingly evident that phenomenologists, like Dewey, seek to elaborate a rich theory of experience that escapes the dilemmas of rigid dualisms and dichotomies. The concept of the *lebenswelt,* which has been important in recent phenomenological investigation, bears a strong resemblance to Dewey's concept of the situation as the basic unit of experience. It is too simple and misleading to declare that "they" are both saying the same thing. But there is a common platform on which there can be a fruitful dialogue between Dewey and phenomenology, a dialogue that could enrich both the phenomenological and the pragmatic traditions.

The fourth major aspect of the contemporary American scene is the persistence of speculative metaphysics. Undaunted by the criticism of metaphysics by positivists, linguistic analysts, and existentialists, metaphysicians have attempted to achieve a comprehensive metaphysical vision of man and the cosmos. This approach has not been widespread, but its spokesmen have been bold and articulate. The metaphysical approach has bypassed Dewey and drawn its major inspiration from Whitehead. It is Whitehead's students who have been America's most notable metaphysicians, although Charles Hartshorne and Paul Weiss, two of the most prominent metaphysicians, were exposed to pragmatism when they edited Peirce's collected papers. The metaphysical aspects of Dewey's work have been almost totally ignored. John Herman Randall is the most notable exception, as a philosopher who has seen the importance of Dewey's metaphysics and who has attempted to develop Dewey's metaphysical suggestions.[2] The neglect of Dewey's metaphysics has been unfortunate because many philosophers have thereby ignored the comprehensive theory of experience and nature that is the background for his more popular investigations.

At the same time, it must be admitted that Dewey was a half-hearted metaphysician. He never really made up his mind whether metaphysics is a specific discipline with its own distinctive aims and approach. He tells us that metaphysics is descriptive and hypothetical, and that it is based on a generalization of those features of nature discovered by scientific procedures. But the line of demarcation between science in its most generalized form and metaphysics is never really clear. The consequences of this uncertainty are serious for Dewey's entire philosophy. Many of his most basic categories are left in "limbo." Such key concepts as quality and continuity, which play such a fundamental role throughout his philosophy, suffer from ambiguity and a lack of clarity. I have argued elsewhere that there is a deep split in Dewey's metaphysics between what might be called a phenomenological strain that focuses on man's encounters, and a realistic strain that attempts to work out the categories of nature where man is continuous with the rest of nature.[3] These two viewpoints need not be incompatible, and Dewey thought that he could assimilate both in a comprehensive theory of experience and nature. But in the final analysis, I do not think that Dewey really succeeded in combining the two approaches in a single comprehensive framework. We are left with suggestions and hints, not carefully elaborated ideas. The difficulties can be seen in what is undoubtedly the most fundamental principle in Dewey—the principle of continuity. It is the heart of his naturalism. We are constantly told that while there are differences and unique patterns of behavior, there are no "breaks" or "jumps" requiring the use of nonnatural categories. What precisely is the meaning and the status of this principle of continuity? Sometimes Dewey speaks as if it were a regulative principle for all inquiry, and sometimes he talks as if it were a generalized conclusion from science. It could, of course, be both, but Dewey has not shown this. We are never given a detailed, systematic analysis of "continuity." Too frequently, Dewey appears to be guilty of the sin that he detected so clearly in others—confusing metaphysics with morals. The principle of continuity has more of an emotive or normative meaning than a descriptive, informative meaning. It is used, without sufficient warrant, to condemn those who introduce "discontinuities" or nonnatural categories. As a result, even the broad term "naturalism" frequently has a normative force rather than an informative meaning. It is never quite clear what would be a nonnatural transaction, and why such transactions are "illegitimate."

No attempt to view Dewey from the perspective of what has come after him would be complete without considering what has happened to the social sciences and education, the disciplines in which philosophy as reconstruction was supposed to have its most direct consequences. The situation here is certainly bleak from Dewey's point of view. In Dewey's outlook, the social sciences were always allied with social recon-

struction. He recognized, of course, the autonomy of any scientific discipline, that it has its own techniques, procedures, and aims. Nevertheless he believed and hoped that as our knowledge of human nature increased, this knowledge would have a direct effect on the formulation of ends-in-view and the means for achieving humanly desirable goods. But the sad fact is that as these disciplines have developed, they have become jealous of their "autonomy." The function of social science, it is claimed, is to achieve theoretical understanding. It is somebody else's function to use and apply the results of these investigations. The result of this attitude of divided function has frequently led to a perversion of the spirit of social science. The knowledge gained from the study of psychology, sociology, and politics has been misused to achieve the undesirable ends of special-interest groups in our society. Instead of the social sciences being used to close the gap between theory and practice, they have been used to widen the gap. Dewey long ago saw the dangers of such a division of labor. Knowledge is power, and power can be used for good or evil. The crisis resulting from the divorce between scientific inquiry and knowledge and its application to our moral and social problems is even greater today than when Dewey lived. One can, however, hope and work toward the realization of the end-in-view that Dewey took to be fundamental for the democratic community—the application and penetration of the scientific spirit in all forms of moral and social life. In this task, social scientists have a major role to play. It ought to be their responsibility to unite theory and practice, to help make the knowledge gained through the study of man and society relevant to solving the problems of man and achieving humanly desirable ends.

Education is the field in which Dewey is supposed to have had the greatest influence and it is here that he has been subjected to vociferous attacks. But the spirit of Dewey's philosophy of education is as relevant now as it ever was. Distinguishing Dewey's philosophy of education from the current distortions of it, we have emphasized that deliberate education is the medium for the reconstruction of experience—a reconstruction from crude, immature, undisciplined experience toward experience funded with intelligence and value. It has unfortunately become fashionable to rigidify Dewey's flexible approach and decry his supposedly all-pervasive influence. Now we are seemingly more hard-headed and "realistic" in our approach to education. New techniques are emphasized—especially in the teaching of science and mathematics. In a post-Sputnik era we have become alarmed that we are not "turning out" enough first-rate scientists and engineers. But we seem to have lost sight of what Dewey said so well—that all education, for better or worse, is moral education.

Bluntly, the success of Dewey's philosophy of education depends on discovering the specific means for fostering creative intelligence. Dewey failed to spell out this technique in detailed and rigorous ways. In part, this is due to his failure to develop systematically his underlying psychological principles. The result has been, especially among those who think of themselves as followers of Dewey, that mehods that were proposed in a tentative, experimental spirit have been treated as if they were ends in themselves.

The divorce between ends and means that Dewey attacked has become all too prevalent in recent thinking about education. We want our children to learn science and mathematics in better and more effective ways, and we are discovering better ways of doing this. But what is our ultimate purpose, what are we trying to achieve in our schools? Too frequently these questions are not discussed, or their answers are thought to be self-evident. But they are not self-evident. The neglect of these issues can easily lead to a school system in which we turn out narrowly trained specialists who do not have a sense of responsibility and commitment for applying scientific intelligence to the problems of life. There is no point in decrying specialization in favor of some vague ideal of the well-rounded man. The pursuit of knowledge demands specialization, and a realistic attitude toward education will face up to this demand. Nevertheless, something more is needed: a clear sense of purpose and goal, an end-in-view. The problem for us today is not so much a matter of increasing our knowledge, but increasing our practical wisdom. The challenge has become even greater to reshape our educational institutions so that creative intelligence will be concretely realized and the values of the democratic community genuinely shared. In "Creative Democracy—The Task Before Us," Dewey has told us that "faith in democracy is all one with faith in experience and education." He sums up the import of democracy as a moral ideal when he says:

> Democracy as compared with other ways of life is the sole way of living which believes wholeheartedly in the process of experience as end and as means; as that which is capable of generating the science which is the sole dependable authority for the direction of further experience and which

> releases emotions, needs, and desires so as to call into being the things that have not existed in the past. For every way of life that fails in its democracy limits the contacts, the exchanges, the communications, the interactions by which experience is steadied while it is also enlarged and enriched. The task of this release and enrichment is one that has to be carried on day by day. Since it is one that can have no end till experience itself comes to an end, the task of democracy is forever that of the creation of a freer and more humane experience in which all share and to which all contribute.[4]

Nothing that has occurred since Dewey wrote this vitiates this ideal. It is still our task to work toward this ideal. Recent events, both national and international, make this task more vital.

Throughout this study, I have sought to avoid two extremes that have been prevalent in the appraisal of Dewey's philosophy—slavish adherence to every word of Dewey as if it were the gospel truth, and total uninformed condemnation. Dewey failed in serious ways. In this final chapter I have suggested some of them. It would be antithetical to the entire spirit of his philosophy not to admit these failures. Philosophy dies when we no longer engage in criticism. Philosophy is, as Dewey has told us, a form of criticism, and the critical task is never completed. At the same time I hope that I have helped to eliminate some of the myths, illusions, and caricatures that have blinded many from seeing the power, vitality, and humaneness of the man and his thought. Sentimental nostalgia has never advanced philosophic inquiry, but all of us, philosophers and others, can learn a great deal from Dewey in the perennial task of seeking a comprehensive vision and understanding of man and his place in the universe.

BIBLIOGRAPHICAL NOTE

John Dewey was a prolific writer. His publications span a period of 70 years, and the complete list of his writings takes up 153 pages of text. The most valuable bibliographical source is Milton H. Thomas, *John Dewey: A Centennial Bibliography* (Chicago: University of Chicago Press, 1962). There are a number of features that make this an extremely useful book. The first part consists of an exhaustive listing of Dewey's writings, arranged in chronological order. Thomas has also listed reviews of Dewey's books, so that the reader is able to discover the immediate reactions to Dewey's publications. The second part consists of a comprehensive listing of works on Dewey, including many unpublished theses. Consequently this volume provides the best means for discovering what Dewey wrote and what has been written about him.

A less comprehensive bibliography of Dewey's writing is to be found in *The Philosophy of John Dewey,* edited by Paul A. Schlipp (Evanston: Northwestern University Press, 1939), pp. 611-676. This volume is the first in the series, "The Library of Living Philosophers." The volume includes a short biography of Dewey written by his daughters and edited by Jane M. Dewey. Also included are a number of critical appraisals of various aspects of Dewey's philosophy and Dewey's response to his critics.

Fortunately, many of Dewey's most important books are now easily available in paperback. These include: *Art as Experience* (Capricorn Books); *The Child and the Curriculum* & *The School and Society* (Phoenix Books); *A Common Faith* (Yale Paperbacks); *Democracy and Education* (Macmillan Paperbacks); *Experience and Education* (Collier Books); *Experience and Nature* (Dover Publications); *Experience and Nature* (revised edition) (Open Court Publishing Co.); *Freedom and Culture* (Capricorn Books); *Individualism: Old and New* (Capricorn Books); *Liberalism and Social Action* (Capricorn Books); *Moral Principles in Education* (Wisdom Library Paperbacks); *Philosophy of Education* (Littlefield, Adams & Co.); *The Public and its Problems* (Swallow Paperbooks); *The Quest for Certainty* (Capricorn Books); *Reconstruction in Philosophy* (Beacon Press); *Theory of Moral Life* (Holt, Rinehart & Winston); John Dewey and Arthur Bentley, *Knowing and the Known* (Beacon Press); John Dewey and Evelyn Dewey, *Schools of Tomorrow* (Dutton Everyman Paperbacks). In addition, *Human Nature and Conduct* is available in a Modern Library edition.

Throughout this study, I have made extensive use of Dewey's essays collected and reprinted in *John Dewey: On Experience, Nature, and Freedom,* which I edited (New York: Liberal Arts Press, 1960). This anthology includes Dewey's autobiographical essay, "From Absolutism to Experimentalism," a number of his most important late papers, and an introduction which gives a condensed overview of his theory of experience and nature.

There are numerous secondary writings on Dewey.

For a comprehensive list, see Milton Thomas' bibliography mentioned above. Some of the most helpful are:

1. George R. Geiger, *John Dewey in Perspective* (New York: Oxford University Press, 1958). Written at the time of the centennial commemoration of Dewey's birth, this is a very sympathetic and judicious presentation of Dewey's leading ideas. Geiger is one of the major commentators who has enabled us to see the importance of the esthetic dimension of experience in Dewey's philosophy. Consequently, it serves as a corrective to narrow and distorted interpretations of Dewey's ideas.

2. Sidney Hook, *John Dewey, An Intellectual Portrait* (New York: The John Day Company, 1939). Hook has been one of Dewey's most dedicated students and one of the most articulate defenders of pragmatism. His book is truly a portrait, and it conveys a very vivid sense of Dewey as a man and a philosopher.

3. Robert J. Roth, S. J., *John Dewey and Self-Realization* (Englewood Cliffs, N.J.: Prentice-Hall, Inc., 1963). One of the most recent interpreters of Dewey's philosophy, Roth argues that the central and dominating theme of Dewey's philosophy is self-realization through interaction with nature. Roth also emphasizes the esthetic dimension of experience and shows its significance for inquiry and technology. Some of his claims about Dewey's concept of religious experience are questionable, but this serves to make this informative book provocative.

4. *John Dewey and the Experimental Spirit in Philosophy,* edited by Charles W. Hendel (New York: Liberal Arts Press, 1959). This volume consists of four lectures delivered at Yale University commemorating the hundredth anniversary of the birth of John Dewey. The contributors are: Charles W. Hendel, Nathaniel

M. Lawrence, Richard J. Bernstein, and John E. Smith. The lectures treat various aspects of Dewey's philosophy including his relation to the empirical tradition, his educational philosophy, his theory of knowledge and value, and his theory of experience.

In addition to the above books about Dewey, a very stimulating overview of American philosophy has recently been published. See John E. Smith, *The Spirit of American Philosophy* (New York: Oxford University Press, 1963). In addition to Smith's excellent chapter on Dewey, this book is most helpful for appreciating Dewey's place in American Philosophy.

NOTES

Chapter 1

1. John Dewey, "Philosophy and Civilization," *Philosophy and Civilization* (New York: Minton, Balch and Company, 1931), p. 5.
2. *Ibid.,* p. 7.
3. *Ibid.,* p. 10.
4. *Ibid.,* p. 9.
5. Dewey, *Experience and Nature* (Chicago, London: Open Court Publishing Company, 1925), p. 402.
6. *Ibid.,* p. 411.
7. Richard McKeon (ed.), *Introduction to Aristotle* (New York: The Modern Library, 1947), p. 429.
8. Dewey, *Democracy and Education* (New York: The Macmillan Company, 1916), p. v.
9. Dewey, "The Development of American Philosophy," *Philosophy and Civilization,* pp. 32–33.

Chapter 2

1. Morris Cohen, *American Thought: A Critical Sketch* (Glencoe, Illinois: The Free Press, 1954), pp. 258–59.
2. Philip P. Wiener, (ed.), *Values in a Universe of Chance: Selected Writings of Charles S. Peirce* (Garden

City, N.Y.: Doubleday & Company, Inc., 1958; a Doubleday Anchor paperback), p. 334.

3. John Dewey, "From Absolutism to Experimentalism," in Richard J. Bernstein (ed.), *John Dewey on Experience, Nature, and Freedom* (New York: Liberal Arts Press, 1960; a Library of Liberal Arts paperback), p. 4. Reprinted from George Plimpton Adams and William Pepperell Montague (eds.), *Contemporary American Philosophy: Personal Statements* (New York: The Macmillan Company, 1930), II, pp. 13–27.

4. *Ibid.,* pp. 10–11.

5. Dewey, "The New Psychology," *Andover Review,* II (September, 1884), p. 288.

6. From a letter published in Robert Mark Wenley, *The Life and Work of George Sylvester Morris* (New York: The Macmillan Company, 1917), pp. 316–17.

7. Dewey, "The Present Position of Logical Theory," *Monist,* II (October, 1891), p. 10.

8. Granville Stanley Hall, review of Dewey's *Psychology,* in *American Journal of Psychology,* I (November, 1887), pp. 154–59.

9. Dewey, "The Reflex Arc Concept in Psychology," *Psychological Review,* III (July, 1896), pp. 357–70.

10. *Ibid.,* p. 361.

11. *Ibid.,* p. 358.

12. *Ibid.,* p. 361.

13. *Ibid.,* p. 363.

14. *Ibid.,* p. 365.

15. Dewey is careful to point out, "I am not raising the question as to how far this teleology is real in any one of these cases; real or unreal, my point holds equally well. It is only when we regard the sequence of acts *as if* they were adapted to reach some end that it occurs to us to speak of one as stimulus and the other as response." *Ibid.,* p. 366, note 1.

16. *Ibid.,* pp. 368–69.

17. *Ibid.,* p. 370.

18. Dewey, "Experience, Knowledge and Value: A Re-

joinder," in Paul Arthur Schilpp (ed.), *The Philosophy of John Dewey* (Evanston and Chicago: Northwestern University Press, 1939; New York: Tudor Publishing Company, 1951), p. 544.

Chapter 3

1. John Dewey, "From Absolutism to Experimentalism," in Richard J. Bernstein (ed.), *John Dewey on Experience, Nature, and Freedom* (New York: Liberal Arts Press, 1960; a Library of Liberal Arts paperback), p. 13. Reprinted from George Plimpton Adams and William Pepperell Montague (eds.), *Contemporary American Philosophy: Personal Statements* (New York: The Macmillan Company, 1930), II, pp. 13–27.
2. *Ibid.*
3. Lewis S. Feuer, "John Dewey and the Back-to-the-People Movement in American Thought," *Journal of the History of Ideas,* XX (October–December, 1959), p. 545. This article is one of the best sources of information about Dewey's early involvement with social affairs. I have made extensive use of this information in this chapter.
4. George Dykhuisen, "John Dewey: The Vermont Years," *Journal of the History of Ideas,* XX (October–December, 1959), p. 522.
5. Dewey, "From Absolutism to Experimentalism," in Bernstein (ed.), *John Dewey on Experience, Nature, and Freedom,* pp. 11–12.
6. Quoted in Dykhuisen, *op. cit.,* p. 537.
7. *Ibid.,* p. 542.
8. Sidney Hook, *John Dewey: An Intellectual Portrait* (New York: The John Day Company, 1939), pp. 5–6.
9. Ralph B. Perry, *The Thought and Character of William James* (Boston: Little, Brown, and Company, 1935), II, pp. 518–19.
10. *Detroit Tribune,* April 13, 1892.

11. Dewey, "Moral Theory and Practice," *International Journal of Ethics,* I (January, 1891), p. 199.

12. Dewey, "The Realism of Jane Addams," in Jane Addams, *Peace and Bread in Time of War,* Anniversary edition, 1915–1945 (New York: King's Crown Press, 1945), p. xix.

13. Dewey, "From Absolutism to Experimentalism," in Bernstein (ed.), *John Dewey on Experience, Nature, and Freedom,* p. 14.

14. Dewey, *The Child and the Curriculum* (reprinted as a paperback with Dewey's *The School and Society;* Chicago: University of Chicago Press—Phoenix Books, 1956), p. 9.

15. *Ibid.,* p. 17.

16. *Ibid.,* p. 18.

17. *Ibid.,* p. 18.

18. *Ibid.,* p. 13.

19. Dewey, *The School and Society* (reprinted as a paperback with Dewey's *The Child and the Curriculum;* Chicago: University of Chicago Press—Phoenix Books, 1956), p. 14.

20. This quotation is from the history of the Laboratory School, *The Dewey School: The Laboratory School of the University of Chicago 1896–1903,* by Katherine C. Mayhew and Anna C. Edwards (New York: D. Appleton-Century Company, 1936), p. 7.

21. Dewey, *My Pedagogic Creed* (published with Albion W. Small's *The Demands of Sociology upon Pedagogy;* New York: E. L. Kellogg & Company, 1897), pp. 15–16.

22. Dewey, *The School and Society,* p. 29.

Chapter 4

1. John Dewey, "An Empirical Survey of Empiricisms," in Richard J. Bernstein (ed.), *John Dewey on*

Experience, Nature, and Freedom (New York: Liberal Arts Press, 1960; a Library of Liberal Arts paperback), pp. 70–87. Reprinted from *Studies in the History of Ideas,* ed. by the Department of Philosophy of Columbia University (New York: Columbia University Press, 1935), III, pp. 3–22.

2. *Ibid.,* pp. 71–72.

3. Richard McKeon (ed.), *Introduction to Aristotle* (New York: The Modern Library, 1947), pp. 107–8.

4. *Ibid.,* p. 11.

5. Dewey, "An Empirical Survey of Empiricisms," in Bernstein (ed.), *John Dewey on Experience, Nature, and Freedom,* p. 77.

6. *Ibid.,* p. 77.

7. *Ibid.,* p. 78.

8. *Ibid.,* p. 84.

9. *Ibid.,* p. 86.

Chapter 5

1. *The Journal of Philosophy, Psychology and Scientific Methods,* I (January 7, 1904), p. 27.

2. John Dewey, "The Need for a Recovery of Philosophy," in Richard J. Bernstein (ed.), *John Dewey on Experience, Nature, and Freedom* (New York: Liberal Arts Press, 1960; a Library of Liberal Arts paperback), p. 69. Reprinted from Dewey *et al., Creative Intelligence: Essays in the Pragmatic Attitude* (New York: Henry Holt and Company, 1917), pp. 3–69.

3. *Ibid.,* p. 21.

4. *Ibid.,* p. 21.

5. *Ibid.,* p. 23.

6. Dewey, *Essays in Experimental Logic* (Chicago: University of Chicago Press, 1916), p. 2.

7. *Ibid.,* p. 5.

8. *Ibid.,* p. 6.

9. *Ibid.*, p. 11.

10. Dewey, "The Reflex Arc Concept in Psychology," *Psychological Review,* III (July, 1896), pp. 357–70.

11. Dewey, "The Need for a Recovery of Philosophy," in Bernstein (ed.), *John Dewey on Experience, Nature, and Freedom,* p. 23.

12. *Ibid.*

13. David Hume, *A Treatise of Human Nature,* ed. by L. A. Selby-Bigge (Oxford: Clarendon Press, 1896), p. 87.

14. Dewey, "The Need for a Recovery of Philosophy," in Bernstein (ed.), *John Dewey on Experience, Nature, and Freedom,* p. 27.

15. Stuart Hampshire, *Thought and Action* (London: Chatto and Windus, 1959), p. 47.

16. Dewey, "The Need for a Recovery of Philosophy," in Bernstein (ed.), *John Dewey on Experience, Nature, and Freedom,* p. 27.

17. *Ibid.*, p. 28.

18. *Ibid.*, p. 23.

19. I speak of a *tendency* toward particularism in Hume. Unfortunately it has become a dogma of recent interpretations of Hume that his philosophy is atomistic and particularistic. For a scholarly corrective to this dogma, see Charles W. Hendel, *Studies in the Philosophy of David Hume* (Princeton: Princeton University Press, 1925), especially the Supplement and Appendices in the revised edition (Indianapolis and New York: The Bobbs-Merrill Company, Inc., 1963; Library of Liberal Arts series). See Supplement: "On Atomism: A Critique of Hume's First Principles and Method," pp. 379–480; and Appendix IV: "On 'The Nature of Experience' and the Senses in Which It Has Been Considered Normative," pp. 505–9. Dewey himself thought that the "truly empirical contribution of Hume lay in his revival of the concepts of habit and of custom and their importance" (Dewey, "An Empirical Survey of Empiricisms," in Bernstein (ed), *John Dewey on Experience, Nature, and Freedom,* p. 83).

See also Dewey's Foreword to the Modern Library edition of his *Human Nature and Conduct* (New York: The Modern Library, 1930).

20. Dewey, *Logic: The Theory of Inquiry* (New York: Henry Holt and Company, 1938), p. 533.

21. Dewey, "Experience, Knowledge and Value: A Rejoinder," in Paul Arthur Schilpp (ed.), *The Philosophy of John Dewey* (Evanston and Chicago: Northwestern University Press, 1939; New York: Tudor Publishing Company, 1951), p. 544.

22. Dewey, "The Need for a Recovery of Philosophy," in Bernstein (ed.), *John Dewey on Experience, Nature, and Freedom,* p. 23.

23. *Ibid.,* p. 34.

24. *Ibid.,* p. 68.

25. *Ibid.*

Chapter 6

1. See *Not Guilty. Report of the Commission of Inquiry into the Charges Made against Leon Trotsky in the Moscow Trials* (New York, London: Harper and Brothers, 1938).

2. See John Dewey and Horace M. Kallen (eds.), *The Bertrand Russell Case* (New York: The Viking Press, 1941).

3. Letter to the Editor, *The New York Times,* June 29, 1949.

4. Throughout this study we have indicated some basic similarities between the spirit of Aristotle and that of Dewey. For a further exploration of these similarities, see John Herman Randall, Jr., *Aristotle* (New York: Columbia University Press, 1960).

5. Dewey, "The New Psychology," *Andover Review,* II (September, 1884), p. 288.

6. G. W. F. Hegel, *The Phenomenology of Mind,* trans.

James B. Baillie (2nd ed., London: G. Allen & Unwin; New York: The Macmillan Company, 1961), p. 144.

7. Dewey, *Essays in Experimental Logic* (Chicago: University of Chicago Press, 1916), p. 1.

8. Dewey, *Experience and Nature* (revised ed.; New York: W. W. Norton & Company, Inc., 1929), p. 4a.

9. *Ibid.*, p. 3a.

10. John Dewey and Arthur F. Bentley, *Knowing and the Known* (Boston: The Beacon Press, 1949).

11. Dewey, letter to Robert V. Daniels, reprinted in "Letters of John Dewey to Robert V. Daniels, 1946–1950," *Journal of the History of Ideas,* XX (October–December, 1959), pp. 569–76.

12. Richard McKeon (ed.), *Introduction to Aristotle* (New York: The Modern Library, 1947), p. 116.

13. *Ibid.*

14. Sir Isaac Newton, *Opticks: or, a Treatise of the Reflections, Refractions, Inflections, and Colours of Light* (3rd ed.; London: Printed for William and John Innys, 1721), pp. 375–76.

15. James Clerk Maxwell, *Matter and Motion* (London, Society for Promoting Christian Knowledge, 1876), pp. 33–34.

16. Dewey, *Experience and Nature* (Chicago, London: Open Court Publishing Company, 1925), p. 253.

17. *Ibid.*, p. 254.

18. *Ibid.*, p. 261.

Chapter 7

1. Alfred North Whitehead, *Science and the Modern World* (New York: The Macmillan Company, 1926), pp. 79–80.

2. Henri Bergson, *An Introduction to Metaphysics,* trans. T. E. Hulme (2nd ed.; New York: Liberal Arts Press, 1955; a Library of Liberal Arts paperback), p. 51.

3. *Ibid.*, pp. 23–24.

4. Arthur O. Lovejoy, *The Reason, the Understanding and Time* (Baltimore: The Johns Hopkins Press, 1961), pp. 47–48.

5. The following few paragraphs are based on my article, "John Dewey's Metaphysics of Experience," *Journal of Philosophy,* LVIII (January 5, 1961), pp. 5–14. This article may also be consulted for a criticism of Dewey's theory of quality.

6. John Dewey, *Experience and Nature* (Chicago, London: Open Court Publishing Company, 1925), p. 259.

7. Dewey, "Peirce's Theory of Quality," in Richard J. Bernstein (ed.), *John Dewey on Experience, Nature, and Freedom* (New York: Liberal Arts Press, 1960; a Library of Liberal Arts paperback), p. 209. Reprinted from *Journal of Philosophy,* XXXII (December 19, 1935), pp. 701–8.

8. Dewey, *Logic: The Theory of Inquiry* (New York: Henry Holt and Company, 1938), p. 68.

9. *Ibid.*, p. 70.

10. Dewey, *Experience and Nature,* p. 85.

11. *Ibid.*

12. Dewey, "Half-Hearted Naturalism," *Journal of Philosophy,* XXIV (February 3, 1927), pp. 60–61.

13. Dewey, *Experience and Nature,* p. 413.

14. *Ibid.*, p. 398 (italics added).

15. *Ibid.*, p. 398.

Chapter 8

1. John Dewey, *Logic: The Theory of Inquiry* (New York: Henry Holt and Company, 1938), p. iii.

2. Dewey, from a letter to Albert G. Balz, reprinted as "In Defense of the Theory of Inquiry," in Richard J. Bernstein (ed.), *John Dewey on Experience, Nature, and Freedom* (New York: Liberal Arts Press, 1960; a Library

of Liberal Arts paperback), p. 135. Reprinted from *Journal of Philosophy,* XLVI (May 26, 1949), pp. 329–42.

3. *Ibid.,* p. 148.

4. Dewey, *Logic: The Theory of Inquiry,* pp. 3–4.

5. *Ibid.,* p. 5.

6. *Ibid.,* p. 104.

7. *Ibid.,* pp. 105–6.

8. *Ibid.,* p. 106.

9. *Ibid.,* p. 105.

10. Dewey, "Qualitative Thought," in Richard J. Bernstein (ed.), *John Dewey on Experience, Nature, and Freedom* (New York: Liberal Arts Press, 1960; a Library of Liberal Arts paperback), p. 198. Reprinted from *The Symposium,* I (January, 1930), pp. 5–32.

11. Dewey, *Logic: The Theory of Inquiry,* p. 107.

12. Dewey, *The Quest for Certainty* (New York: Minton, Balch and Company, 1929), p. 228.

13. Dewey, *Logic: The Theory of Inquiry,* p. 111.

14. For the new emphasis on inquiry and the functional status of distinctions, see N. R. Hanson, *Patterns of Discovery: An Inquiry into the Conceptual Foundations of Science* (Cambridge, Eng.: Cambridge University Press, 1958), and P. K. Feyerabend, "Explanation, Reduction, and Empiricism," in Herbert Feigl and Grover Maxwell (eds.), *Scientific Explanation, Space, and Time* (*Minnesota Studies in the Philosophy of Science,* Vol. III [Minneapolis: University of Minnesota Press, 1962]). Feyerabend's extensive notes and references as well as many other papers in the three volumes of the *Minnesota Studies* provide further evidence of this "new" Deweyean approach. See also the concluding chapter of this study.

15. Dewey, *Logic: The Theory of Inquiry,* p. 112.

16. *Ibid.,* pp. 112–13.

17. *Ibid.,* pp. 113–14.

18. For an illuminating discussion of Dewey's doctrine of knowledge as the warranted end-product of inquiry and the relation of this doctrine to contemporary discussions

of truth, see Gertrude Ezorsky, "Truth in Context," *Journal of Philosophy,* LX (February 28, 1963), pp. 113–35.

19. Wilfred Sellars, "Empiricism and Philosophy of the Mind," in Herbert Feigl and Michael Scriven (eds.), *The Foundations of Science and the Concepts of Psychology and Psychoanalysis* (*Minnesota Studies in the Philosophy of Science,* Vol. I [Minneapolis: University of Minnesota Press, 1956]). There are many features in Sellars' philosophy that take up Deweyean themes, developing them in new and novel ways. Consequently, both the similarities and differences between Sellars and Dewey are highly instructive. See Wilfred Sellars, *Science, Perception and Reality* (London: Routledge & Kegan Paul; New York: The Humanities Press, 1963).

Chapter 9

1. John Dewey, *The Influence of Darwin on Philosophy and Other Essays in Contemporary Thought* (New York: Henry Holt and Company, 1910), pp. 8–9.

2. Dewey, *Reconstruction in Philosophy* (New York: Henry Holt and Company, 1920), pp. 75–76.

3. Dewey, *Theory of Valuation* (Chicago: University of Chicago Press, 1939), p. 31.

4. Dewey, "The Logic of Judgments of Practice," in *Essays in Experimental Logic* (Chicago: University of Chicago Press, 1916), p. 335.

5. *Ibid.,* p. 368.

6. Dewey, *Reconstruction in Philosophy,* pp. 163–64.

7. Dewey, "The Objects of Valuation," *Journal of Philosophy,* XV (May 9, 1918), p. 257.

8. John Dewey and James H. Tufts, *Ethics* (New York: Henry Holt and Company, 1908), p. 323.

9. For a further discussion of these issues and the way in which the situation provides the normative context for valuation and decision, see Sidney Hook, "The Desirable

and Emotive in Dewey's Ethics," in Sidney Hook (ed.), *John Dewey: Philosopher of Science and Freedom. A Symposium* (New York: The Dial Press, 1950), pp. 194–216.

10. Dewey, *Human Nature and Conduct* (New York: The Modern Library, 1930), p. 255.

11. Dewey, *Reconstruction in Philosophy,* p. 164.

Chapter 10

1. Charles S. Peirce, "Questions Concerning Faculties Claimed for Man," "Some Consequences of Four Incapacities," and "Grounds of Validity of the Laws of Logic: Further Consequences of Four Incapacities," in Charles Hartshorne and Paul Weiss (eds.), *Collected Papers of Charles Sanders Peirce,* Vol. V, *Pragmatism and Pragmaticism* (Cambridge, Mass.: Harvard University Press, 1934).

2. See my article, "Peirce's Theory of Perception," in Edward C. Moore and Richard S. Robin (eds.), *Studies in the Philosophy of Charles Sanders Peirce: Second Series* (Amherst, Mass.: University of Massachusetts Press, 1964).

3. Philip P. Wiener, (ed.), *Values in a Universe of Chance: Selected Writings of Charles S. Peirce* (Garden City, N.Y.: Doubleday & Company, Inc., 1958; a Doubleday Anchor paperback), p. 69.

4. For an analysis of the role of the community in Royce's philosophy, see John Edwin Smith, *Royce's Social Infinite: The Community of Interpretation* (New York: Liberal Arts Press, 1950).

5. John Dewey, *Experience and Nature* (Chicago, London: Open Court Publishing Company, 1925), p. 166.

6. Dewey, "The Inclusive Philosophic Idea," *Philosophy and Civilization* (New York: Minton, Balch and Company, 1931), p. 80.

7. *Ibid.,* p. 86.

8. Dewey, *Experience and Nature,* pp. 204–5.

9. Dewey, *Democracy and Education* (New York: The Macmillan Company, 1916), p. 101.

10. *Ibid.,* p. 100.

11. Dewey, "Creative Democracy—The Task Before Us," in Max H. Fisch (ed.), *Classic American Philosophers* (New York: Appleton-Century-Crofts, Inc., 1951), p. 393.

12. Dewey, *Freedom and Culture* (New York: G. P. Putnam's Sons, 1939), p. 102.

13. *Ibid.,* p. 148.

14. Robert J. Roth, S. J., *John Dewey and Self-Realization* (Englewood Cliffs, N.J.: Prentice-Hall, Inc., 1963; paperback), p. 4.

15. Dewey, "Creative Democracy—The Task Before Us," in Max H. Fisch (ed.), *Classic American Philosophers,* p. 390.

16. Dewey, *Freedom and Culture,* p. 148.

17. Dewey, "Philosophies of Freedom," in Richard J. Bernstein (ed.), *John Dewey on Experience, Nature, and Freedom* (New York: Liberal Arts Press, 1960; a Library of Liberal Arts paperback), p. 265. Reprinted from Horace Meyer Kallen (ed.), *Freedom in the Modern World* (New York: Coward-McCann, 1928), pp. 236–71.

18. *Ibid.,* p. 265.

19. *Ibid.,* p. 266.

20. *Ibid.,* p. 267.

21. Dewey, *Individualism, Old and New* (New York: Minton, Balch and Company, 1930), p. 168.

22. Dewey, "Philosophies of Freedom," in Bernstein (ed.), *John Dewey on Experience, Nature, and Freedom,* p. 271.

23. *Ibid.,* p. 276.

24. *Ibid.,* pp. 286–87.

25. Dewey, *Democracy and Education,* p. 383.

26. Dewey, *Construction and Criticism* (New York: Columbia University Press, 1930), p. 11; Dewey, "Indi-

viduality and Experience," *Journal of the Barnes Foundation,* II (January, 1926), p. 1.

27. Dewey, *Democracy and Education,* p. 24.

28. *Ibid.,* p. 24.

Chapter 11

1. Stephen C. Pepper, "Some Questions on Dewey's Esthetics," in Paul Arthur Schilpp (ed.), *The Philosophy of John Dewey* (Evanston and Chicago: Northwestern University Press, 1939; New York: Tudor Publishing Company, 1951), p. 372.

2. John Dewey, *Experience and Nature* (Chicago, London: Open Court Publishing Company, 1925), p. 355.

3. *Ibid.,* p. 90.

4. *Ibid.,* p. 90.

5. *Ibid.,* pp. 94–95.

6. *Ibid.,* p. 96.

7. *Ibid.,* p. 358.

8. Dewey, *Art as Experience* (New York: Minton, Balch and Company, 1934), p. 40.

9. Dewey, *The Quest for Certainty* (New York: Minton, Balch and Company, 1929), p. 235.

10. Dewey, *Experience and Nature,* pp. 373–74.

11. *Ibid.,* p. 368.

12. For an excellent discussion of this point, see Sidney Hook, "The Desirable and Emotive in Dewey's Ethics," in Sidney Hook (ed.), *John Dewey: Philosopher of Science and Freedom. A Symposium* (New York: The Dial Press, 1950), pp. 197 ff.

13. Dewey, *Experience and Nature,* p. 367.

14. *Ibid.,* p. 358.

15. Dewey, *Art as Experience,* pp. 132–33.

16. *Ibid.,* p. 107.

17. *Ibid.,* p. 105.

18. Irwin Edman, "Dewey and Art," in Sidney Hook

(ed.), *John Dewey: Philosopher of Science and Freedom. A Symposium,* pp. 62–63.

19. Dewey, *Art as Experience,* p. 347.
20. *Ibid.,* p. 348.
21. *Ibid.*
22. Dewey, "Philosophy and Civilization," *Philosophy and Civilization* (New York: Minton, Balch and Company, 1931), p. 12.
23. Dewey, "From Absolutism to Experimentalism," in Richard J. Bernstein (ed.), *John Dewey on Experience, Nature, and Freedom* (New York: Liberal Arts Press, 1960; a Library of Liberal Arts paperback), pp. 6–7. Reprinted from George Plimpton Adams and William Pepperell Montague (eds.), *Contemporary American Philosophy: Personal Statements* (New York: The Macmillan Company, 1930), II, pp. 13–27.
24. *Ibid.,* p. 11.
25. *Ibid.*
26. Dewey, *A Common Faith* (New Haven: Yale University Press, 1934), p. 9.
27. *Ibid.,* pp. 31–32.
28. *Ibid.,* p. 13.
29. *Ibid.,* p. 19.
30. *Ibid.,* p. 33.
31. *Ibid.,* pp. 50–51.
32. *Ibid.,* p. 25.
33. *Ibid.,* p. 25.
34. *Ibid.,* p. 87.

Chapter 12

1. John Dewey, "Experience, Knowledge and Value: A Rejoinder," in Paul Arthur Schilpp (ed.), *The Philosophy of John Dewey* (Evanston and Chicago: Northwestern University Press, 1939; New York: Tudor Publishing Company, 1951), p. 554.

2. John Herman Randall, Jr., *Nature and Historical Experience: Essays in Naturalism and in the Theory of History* (New York: Columbia University Press, 1958).

3. Richard J. Bernstein, "John Dewey's Metaphysics of Experience," *Journal of Philosophy,* LVIII (January 5, 1961), pp. 5–14.

4. Dewey "Creative Democracy—The Task Before Us," in Max H. Fisch (ed.), *Classic American Philosophers* (New York: Appleton-Century-Crofts, Inc., 1951), p. 394.

INDEX

Index